☐ O U T O F T H E ☐

R O U G H

☐ J A M E S D Y E T ☐

THOMAS NELSON PUBLISHERS
Nashville • Atlanta • London • Vancouver

*To my wife, Gloria; my son, Brian; my daughters, Sherrie and
Heather; and my sons-in-law, Jim and Brad.
They have contributed much to my golf collection—and infinitely
more to my life.*

*Also, to Joe Ragont, my Illinois golf buddy, who encouraged me in
the writing of this book.*

Copyright © 1996 by James T. Dyet

Published in Nashville, Tennessee, by Thomas Nelson, Inc., and distributed in
Canada by Word Communications, Ltd., Richmond, British Columbia, and in the
United Kingdom by Word (UK), Ltd., Milton Keynes, England.

Scripture quotations are from the NEW KING JAMES VERSION of the Bible.
Copyright © 1979, 1980, 1982, Thomas Nelson, Inc., Publishers.

Library of Congress Cataloging-in-Publication Data

Dyet, James T.
    Out of the rough / Jim Dyet.
    p.cm.
    ISBN 0-7852-7659-9 (cb)
    1. Golfers—Religious life. 2. Golf—Religious aspects—Christianity. 3. Golf—
Anecdotes. I. Title.
BV4596.G64D84   1996
242'.68—dc20   96-6444
                                                                CIP

Printed in the United States of America
2 3 4 5 6 7 - 02 01 00 99 98 97 96

CONTENTS

Course Number 1: Eagle Heights

The Front Nine

The Back Nine

Course Number 2: Desert Springs

The Front Nine

The Back Nine

Course Number 3: Singing Hills

The Front Nine

The Back Nine

Course Number 4: Pleasant Meadows

The Front Nine

The Back Nine

Course Number 1:
Eagle Heights

Even the youths shall faint and be weary,
And the young men shall utterly fall,
But those who wait on the LORD
Shall renew their strength;
They shall mount up with wings like eagles,
They shall run and not be weary,
They shall walk and not faint.
Isaiah 40:30-31

1 ❑ GETTING a FIRM GRIP on LIFE

A good grip on a golf club doesn't guarantee par golf, but it sure helps to keep triple bogeys at bay.

Most golfers use the overlapping grip. Some, however, prefer the interlocking grip; others, the baseball grip; and a few—those who walk on the wild side—the cross grip. In recent years the cross grip has become popular as a putting grip with a growing number of golfers. Putting seems to be the most "let's-try-something-different" part of golf. Perhaps someday we'll all find something that solves our putting woes!

Thousands of errant shots, embarrassing scores, and even airborne golf clubs may be traced to an uneducated grip. Even graphite shafts and properly weighted clubheads can't offset the negative consequences of an improper grip.

Although each golfer must find the grip that's right for him or her, many seasoned golfers recommend the overlapping grip, with the V formed by the thumb and forefinger of the right hand pointing to the chin and the V formed by the thumb and forefinger of the left hand pointing to the right eye. The next step is to grip the club firmly but gently.

In life, as well as in golf, a good sense of direction and control starts with a proper grip. "Test all things; hold fast what is good. Abstain from every form of evil," the apostle Paul wrote in 1 Thessalonians 5:21-22. Then, in 1 Timothy 6:12, he urged his young protégé Timothy to "lay hold on eternal life, to which you were also called and have confessed the good confession in the presence of many witnesses."

Thank God for His Word, the Bible, and for its unfailing promise of eternal life. Thank Him, too, for the Bible's clear guidelines for successful living. Ask for His help in avoiding hazards. Face today's challenges with a firm grip on the faith.

A good way to get a grip on life is to recognize that the Lord has a grip on everything—including you. Read John 10:27-29.

2 ❏ CHECK YOUR STANCE

Smack a ball with your feet too close together, and don't be surprised to see it zoom low over the fairway. It may just kiss the grass and die a hundred yards out. On the other hand, if you hit a shot with your feet spread too wide, the ball may sky so high that it almost produces rain. Placing your left foot too far ahead of the right may cause a hook; whereas placing your right foot too far ahead of the left may cause a slice. A downhill stance contributes to a slice. An uphill stance contributes to a hook.

Closed stance, open stance, square stance—golf's a tough game! It's often hard to know how to stand and where to stand, but one thing is certain—you have to stand firm. Even the right stance at the right time won't amount to much if you slip during your backswing and enter phase one of a backward somersault. I can speak from experience.

Playing golf one dry January day and wearing sneakers (spikes weren't allowed on the course), I slipped on especially dry grass while hitting my first fairway shot. I recall standing on only one foot when the club made contact with the ball. The result was terrible. Fifty yards closer to the green, I had a similar experience. This time I struck the ball without having either foot on terra firma. Again the ball rolled about fifty yards. I rolled five.

The Christian life is tough too. Jesus said it would be.

At times we face discouragements. Life seems to be an unending succession of downhill lies. At other times what appear to be insurmountable challenges confront us, and life seems to be hand-ing us more than our fair share of uphill lies. Occasionally, however, the ground seems level. But even then, if we fail to stand firmly, we can slip and lose the advantage. If we want to turn in a good round, we must heed the apostle Paul's counsel to "stand fast in the faith" (1 Cor. 16:13), to stand with our waists girded with truth (Eph. 6:14), and to "stand fast in the Lord" (Phil. 4:1).

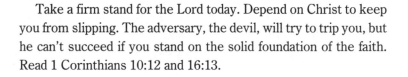

Take a firm stand for the Lord today. Depend on Christ to keep you from slipping. The adversary, the devil, will try to trip you, but he can't succeed if you stand on the solid foundation of the faith. Read 1 Corinthians 10:12 and 16:13.

3 ❏ IT'S the CLUBS—or IS IT?

Graphite shafts; metal woods; cork-filled woods; jumbo drivers such as Big Bertha, Killer Whale, the Judge, the Wave, King Cobra, Big Head, the Launcher, Fat Eddie, and Boom Boom; different drivers/different lofts. State-of-the-art golf clubs draw us to them with an allurement that's hard to resist. We somehow think that the most advanced, best-built woods and irons will shave strokes off our score faster than a sudden cold front drops the temperature in late August. However, deep in our hearts we know good clubs alone can't provide an instant cure for a roundhouse hook, a topped shot, or a wild slice. There is simply no substitute for talent acquired by practice, practice, practice.

Have you surveyed the state-of-the-art helps for Christian living that fill the shelves and display racks in Christian book stores? Literature and audio/video products, attractively designed and well produced, promise help for Christian living. They are not intended, though, to replace the Holy Spirit's power in our lives. As we apply biblical principles in our walk with God and depend on the Holy Spirit for the ability to meet daily challenges, our ability to honor God increases.

A familiar Bible story may help us rivet this truth in our minds.

Before becoming Israel's king, young David showed that dependence upon God's ability is foundational to success. Having been sent by his father to take some food to his three oldest brothers, David arrived at the front line of Israel's army. Israel's arch enemies, the Philistines, were entrenched boldly behind their biggest boaster and Israel's chief intimidator, Goliath. A hulking, nine-foot-tall trash talker, Goliath made the Israelites feel two feet tall by challenging them to send a man to fight him. There were no volunteers—that is, until David arrived!

Believing God would enable him to topple Goliath, David volunteered for the assignment. Reluctantly King Saul agreed and equipped David with his royal armor. David protested because he hadn't had time to test the equipment. So he took off the armor, chose instead his shepherd's staff, a sling, and five smooth stones, and then he confronted Goliath. The result? One small stone, faith, and the power of God combined to mortally wound Goliath (1 Sam. 17:22-50).

Read Galatians 5:16-25 today. Meditate on Zechariah 4:6: "'Not by might nor by power, but by My Spirit,' / Says the LORD of hosts." His ability more than compensates for any disability.

4 ❏ A GREAT RECOVERY SHOT

W e've all been there: behind a tree, in a bunker, in a gully, in deep grass and weeds, in a sand trap. At such times we can decide to sell our clubs at the first opportunity, or we can determine to relax, keep the old head down, and play a recovery shot that our golf buddies will talk about for the rest of the season.

A plaque in a bunker in the rough, off the left side of the seventeenth fairway at Royal Lytham & St. Annes in Blackpool, England, bears silent testimony to a historic and dramatic shot. Playing in the 1926 Open Championship and tied with Al Watrous, Bobby Jones Jr. hit a five iron out of the bunker's sand, carried 170 yards over the rough and landed on the green, inside Watrous's second shot. Jones went on to par the hole. Apparently, Watrous was so unnerved by Jones's recovery shot that he three-putted and lost the championship and its $100,000 prize.

Sometimes, in spite of our best efforts to follow the straight path God has marked for us in His Word, we wander into a bunker, where we feel like giving up. Fortunately, God grants recovery "shots." Our greatest victory may lie just beyond the bunker.

Peter was determined to follow the Lord closely. Courageously, but self-confidently, he boasted that he would never deny the Lord (Matt. 26:35). But later, when the Lord was arrested and subjected to an illegal trial, Peter denied three times that he was one of Jesus' followers. Peter failed to confess Christ even in the presence of a young servant girl (Matt. 26:69-74). Peter had fallen into a "bunker," and he might have been there a long time if our Lord wasn't such a master of "recovery shots."

Following His resurrection, Jesus restored Peter to Himself and commissioned him to feed His sheep (John 21:15-17). Not long after the restoration, Peter preached to a host of Jews on the Day of Pentecost, and three thousand listeners responded by turning to Christ in faith (Acts 2:14-41). Clearly, Peter's greatest victory lay just beyond the bunker!

Hebrews 10:35 cheers us on to victory: "Do not cast away your confidence, which has great reward." No matter how impossible your situation seems today, trust God to turn big obstacles into great opportunities to experience His power. Read Psalm 56 today.

5 ❑ I'D RATHER BE GOLFING

There you were driving to work on a gorgeous day, when a bumper sticker caught your eye. "I'd Rather Be Golfing," it boldly confessed. "Amen," you whispered mournfully. A perfectly natural and innocent response. However, some things are more important than golf, even such unglamorous things as paying bills, feeding, clothing, and educating the kids, keeping the house in good repair, and shopping with your spouse. If someone became so addicted to golf that he quit working and drained his savings to support his habit, he would surely suffer emotionally as well as financially. So would his family.

In Scotland, around A.D. 1430, "golfe" or "the gouf" had become so popular that King James II of Scotland feared the pastime placed the country at risk in its ongoing war with England. He reasoned that his men were spending too much time chasing the "golfe" ball and too little time practicing archery. The Scottish archers would pose little threat to their English foes. (Apparently King James II considered a well-placed clubhead no match for a well-aimed arrow!) The king persuaded his government to pass an act of parliament banning "golfe."

As Christians, our interests must be subservient to our King. Anything that jeopardizes service for the King of kings must be identified and treated as a lower priority. Jesus Himself challenged that "No one, having put his hand to the plow, and looking back, is fit for the kingdom of God" (Luke 9:62). Colossians 3:1-4 nudges us gently but firmly to keep spiritual interests at the top of our list of priorities. Doing so will mean a whole lot now and even more when Christ returns.

Read Colossians 3:1-4. This passage of Scripture urges us to set our focus on heaven's values. Defining the difference between temporal pleasures and eternal priorities can make today eternally worthwhile.

6 ❑ CONSISTENCY

It hurts to admit it, but consistency isn't an identifiable characteristic of my game. However, it used to be. More than forty years ago, when I was a teenager, I played consistently in the high 70s. But, as my wife so often reminds me, "Ol' Man Useto's dead and gone!" Today, I may play a few good holes followed by a string of horrific holes. Of course, now that I'm sixty something (my age, not my score for nine holes), I find that my repertoire of excuses is sixty something too.

I won't share all my excuses with you, but here are a few of my favorites: Haven't played much golf lately. Too much work at the office. Bad back. Bad weather. Bad tee time. Bad toe blister. Bad bounces. Slow traffic getting to the course. Slow foursome in front. Slow greens. Slow digestion. Cheap clubs. Borrowed clubs. New clubs. Too many bunkers. Too many blind holes. Too many bugs. Lost my rhythm. Lost my touch. Lost my coordination. Lost my trusty putter. Lost a spike.

Once, when playing nine holes with my son-in-law Brad, I was even par at the end of seven. Then inconsistency struck like a hurricane. I triple bogeyed the eighth hole and quintuple bogeyed the ninth. Even my repertoire of excuses couldn't help me explain that disaster.

Inconsistency can wreck a streak of Christian living too. Often, about the time we assume that we have mastered the art of walking with God, we blow it. And we can't blame anything or anyone but ourselves. Fortunately, forgiveness is available (1 John 1:9).

Just as scoring well in golf depends on consistent play—one good shot at a time—so scoring well in the Christian life depends on walking with God, one good step at a time.

Read 2 John 4-6. Consistent Christian living involves walking in truth. As we obey God day by day, our love for Him and others stamps our credentials as consistent believers. Make today a no-excuses-necessary kind of day.

7 ❑ SUNDAY GOLF

***

Have you noticed that in the summertime, Sunday seems to be the most glorious day of the week? Monday, Tuesday, Wednesday, and Thursday are often dreary, and Friday is windy. Somehow, Saturday extends the dreariness and winds of the preceding days, adds a torrential downpour, and scorns Saturday golfers.

But when Sunday dawns, the clouds lift, the rain stops, and spectacular sun rays gleam over the eastern horizon. Sunny skies and pleasant conditions are on tap. The air smells fresh and invigorating. A faint scent of fairway grass rides a gentle, warm breeze. Another perfect day for golf!

Sunday beckons golfers to their respective course as alluringly as the Pied Piper of Hamelin beckoned village children. But shouldn't golfers attend church on Sunday?

Perhaps sixteenth-century golfers in Scotland just couldn't resist the appeal of Sunday's best-of-the-week golf weather. Instead of worshiping at their respective kirks, they opted to play their favorite courses. Then the unthinkable happened.

Scotland, golf's birthplace, banned the grand old game. Not entirely, though. A royal proclamation in 1592 restricted golf to six days a week and made Sunday golf as nonexistent in Scotland as a squandered penny. Apparently the king wanted Scots and their pennies to attend church regularly.

Much to the relief of Scottish golfers, the ban was amended in 1618 to allow golf on Sunday if players attended church first.

I doubt if a ban on Sunday golf today would improve church attendance. Despite our love of fairways, greens, long drives, and short putts, we Christian golfers love God more than golf. Our commitment to our great God is far greater than our commitment to the grand old game. Come Sunday, we'll be present for worship.

Read Hebrews 10:24-25. By attending church regularly, we honor God, encourage our fellow Christians, improve our credibility with our neighbors, and strengthen our relationship with God. Another plus for attending church—no tee time is necessary!

8 ❑ A Game of Etiquette

Historically, golf has been known as a game of etiquette. And for good reason. Almost as soon as beginning golfers learn to distinguish a driver from a putter, they discover that golf etiquette obliges them to act politely on the course. Here are some of the rules of etiquette they must honor:

- Don't cheat.
- Remain quiet and motionless when a player addresses his ball.
- Don't laugh—don't even grin—when a player hits a bad shot.
- Replace divots.
- Don't hit out of turn; farthest from the green shoots first.
- The player with the lowest score on a hole hits first off the next tee. (He has the honors.)
- Stand away from a player's line of vision when he hits his ball.
- Don't step on the "line" between a player's ball on a green and the hole.
- If your ball lies in a player's line on a green, remove your ball and mark where it lay.
- Allow a faster group to play through. When all members of your group have reached a par-three green, step behind the green and signal the next group to hit.
- Don't hold up play.

In daily living, as in golf, Christians ought to be courteous. The Bible encourages us to walk as Jesus walked and to put others' interests ahead of our own (Phil. 2:4; 1 Pet. 2:21). Although the Bible doesn't dispense rigid rules for living, it does establish the high standard of love. If we truly love God and our neighbor, we will respect God and others. Our Christian etiquette will flow spontaneously without partiality. Even when we rub shoulders with those whose personalities resemble coarse sandpaper, we will treat them courteously.

Galatians 5:22-23 lists nine characteristics of the fruit of the Spirit. At least three of them—love, kindness, and gentleness—comprise a courtesy fruit basket. Why not deliver courtesy fruit baskets today wherever you go?

9 ❑ ENJOYING the GREAT OUTDOORS

Whether digging divots or driving three hundred yards, today's golfer will tell you a round of golf soothes the troubled mind. And who can dispute the claim? Anyone who spends a couple of hours or more on a golf course finds therapeutic healing there. Somehow, job stress lifts off and flies far away, as if John Daly clobbered it with incredible strength, a flawless swing, and perfect timing. Even a bad score can't erase the relaxation golf provides. "It was fun," you'll hear departing golfers tell one another. "Let's do it again soon."

If you enjoy the great outdoors of nubby green hills, tree-lined fairways, and idyllic blue ponds, you can identify with David, the shepherd lad who became Israel's king. Although he held a shepherd's staff rather than a golf club, David marveled at God's creation. Completing a sweeping gaze of the Judean sky and contemplating the beauty of nature, David reflected, "O LORD, our Lord, / How excellent is Your name in all the earth" (Ps. 8:9).

I have often fantasized about playing golf in my native Scotland. The history, hills, heather, and heath that grace the birthplace and cradle of golf would surely combine to quicken my pulse and refresh my spirit. My fantasy may never become reality, but at least I can always treasure my golf memories formed at North American courses. The courses on this side of the Atlantic may lack heather and heath, but they provide abundant scenic enjoyment.

Golf course designers deserve credit for their uncanny ability to carve beautiful fairways and greens out of hills and valleys, but God deserves our awe and praise for creating those hills and valleys. His creative genius lies behind the breathtaking beauty of New England courses blanketed by fall colors, midwestern courses blessed with ponds and meadows, mountain states courses framed by towering snowcaps, and southwestern courses ringed by palms and bathed in sunshine. No wonder stress lifts and thoughts of divine greatness settle into our souls when we tee up!

Let the scenic surroundings of a golf course transport your thoughts up and away from the frenzied world of such things as spreadsheets, deadlines, sales quotas, and personnel problems and lead you to share David's song of praise: "O LORD, our Lord, / How excellent is Your name in all the earth!"

Take time to smell the roses. Take time also to sense the presence and excellence of the One who created them and their fragrance. Read Psalm 8 today.

10 ❑ GOLF BUDDIES

In 1990 my wife Gloria and I pulled up stakes and moved from Denver to Chicago for a new ministry. We left behind our three grown children, majestic mountains, dry air, dazzling sunshine, our home, nineteen years of memories, familiar surroundings, and good friends.

Long-distance moving is stressful for anybody, but I think it is especially stressful for a golfer. We must say good-bye not only to relatives and friends but also to a special breed of friends—golf buddies. They're the guys who often shuffled with us through knee-deep grass in search of an errant ball. They gave us mulligans just when we needed them most. They granted gimmies, laughed at our jokes, grimaced when we topped our ball, and affirmed our best golf shots.

Buddies like the ones you leave behind when you move are hard to find at the new location. They just don't come running up to the moving van and say, "Hey, I saw a set of golf clubs come off the truck. Want to play in a foursome Saturday morning?" Nor does the Welcome Wagon hostess pull a list of golf buddy names out of her basket and hand it to you with a complimentary greens fee. Uh-uh. Finding new golf buddies takes time and serendipity. But you do find them, and when you do, you feel like you've struck gold!

Christian fellowship is even better than golf fellowship. Of course, if your golf buddies are also Christians, you enjoy a double blessing. Christian friends share life's highest values, strongest convictions, most important beliefs, and a firm commitment to Jesus Christ. They pray when you're burdened, rejoice when you're elated, weep when you're distressed, and lend a helping hand when you're in need. Furthermore, Christian friends are easier to find than golf buddies. Best of all, when you're about to pull up stakes and move to your eternal home, you don't have to say a final good-bye. Heaven is their destination too.

I wonder . . . will there be any golf courses in heaven, where my buddies and I . . .

Take a few moments today to thank God for Christian fellowship. Thank Him for your friends in Christ. Read the apostle Paul's warm greetings to his Christian friends in Rome (Rom. 16:1-16), Corinth (1 Cor. 16:19-23; 2 Cor. 13:11-14), Philippi (Phil. 4:21-23), Colosse (Col. 4:10-15), and Thessalonica (1 Thess. 5:26-28).

Christian fellowship provides the best and longest lasting friendship in the world—and in the next one too!

11 ❑ THE RIGHT CLUB for the RIGHT SHOT

Only a novice would use a three wood to reach the green from fifty yards out, but how often does even an experienced golfer select the wrong club? You've heard the usual laments: "I should have used a four iron. The wind caught my ball and dropped it twenty yards short of the green." "Wow, I overshot the green by at least thirty yards. I thought a seven iron was the right club. I should have used a nine."

No doubt about it, a player can lower his or her score significantly by learning to use the right club for the right shot. Similarly, we believers can turn in better scores in Christian living once we know which Scripture to use in a given situation.

"Take . . . the sword of the Spirit, which is the word of God," Paul wrote in Ephesians 6:17. But what did Paul mean by "the word of God"? Is the believer supposed to battle temptation by thrusting his Bible into the devil's face? No. The word Paul used for *word* in Ephesians 6:17 means a specific word.

Jesus showed us how this principle works. He countered temptation by applying a specific scriptural injunction to each specific evil suggestion the devil offered Him (Matthew 4:1-11). Jesus deflected the temptations by quoting Deuteronomy 8:3, 6:16, and 6:13. The believer who follows Jesus' example will draw from Scripture the specific "word" from God that relates to the temptation he faces. He will obey that specific word, and in dependence on God, he will overcome.

Read Psalm 119:1-11. Memorize verse 11, and count on God's specific words to help you walk with Him and score well in the game of life. When you finish the course God has designed for you, you will be able to echo the words of Psalm 119:111-12: "Your testimonies I have taken as a heritage forever, / For they are the rejoicing of my heart. / I have inclined my heart to perform Your statutes / Forever, to the very end."

12 ❏ WORKING on the SHORT GAME

There ought to be a law—a golf law that states that if you drive over 275 yards straight down the fairway, you can pick up your ball and take a par for the hole or play it and hope for an eagle or a birdie. Given the option, most golfers would probably settle for a par.

You know why, don't you? Horrible things can happen after a beautiful, long, straight tee shot. A topped ball. A shank. A sand-trap burial. A shot that sails over the green, lands on a down slope, and dives for cover into a clump of trees. Three or four putts.

In Christian living, too, it's important to play the short game well. Who wants to begin with a blast only to flub up later in "the short game"? Little things such as controlling one's temper, speaking kind words, filing an accurate tax return, giving an honest day's work, helping someone in need, and treating others lovingly— these short-game challenges can wreck a strong testimony.

Christian character doesn't consist of just one enormous, booming quality, but of several qualities well placed in daily relationships. Galatians 5:22-23 marks them as love, joy, peace, longsuffering, kindness, goodness, faithfulness, gentleness, and sclf-control. These "short-game" factors determine the effectiveness of a believer's witness to Christ.

Read Galatians 5:16-26. What part of "the short game" do you need to work on? Wise King Solomon advised catching the little foxes that ruin the vineyards (Song 2:15). Ask the Lord to help you set a few snares today.

13 ❑ WHEN TEMPER and CLUB GET OUT of HAND

When I was a young caddie at a private course in my hometown, I dreaded being assigned to a golfer unaffectionately dubbed "The Outlaw." So did all the other caddies. Because the caddie shack overlooked the parking lot and we had learned to recognize each member's car, we kept a watchful eye for The Outlaw's arrival. Upon seeing his car enter the lot, a foreboding silence descended over us. At times we bolted from the caddie shack, ran into a nearby wooded area, and waited there until we saw The Outlaw tee off and stomp down the first fairway.

Why did we recoil at the thought of caddying for The Outlaw? He had a violent temper and a wretched golf game. The two combined to make caddying for him exhausting and extremely dangerous. After each bad shot, The Outlaw's temper exploded like misdirected fireworks. Sometimes, with arms flailing and nostrils flaring, he cursed his caddie, accusing him of fidgeting during his backswing. At other times, he was even more volatile; he would throw his club at him. The course should have imposed a hard-hat rule within a fifty-yard radius of The Outlaw's ball.

A hot temper fails to win friends and influence people off the golf course as well as on it. In a fit of jealous rage, Cain killed his brother Abel (Gen. 4:3-8). Anger drove Moses to disobey the Lord at Kadesh, thereby forfeiting for Moses the opportunity to lead the Children of Israel into Canaan (Num. 20:1-12). King Saul's hot temper flared against David when he heard the people of Israel praise David more than him. He hurled a spear at David, hoping to pin him to a wall (1 Sam. 18:8-11). Fuming with rage because the wise men had left the country without disclosing the location of the newborn King of the Jews, King Herod ordered the wholesale massacre of all the infants within his jurisdiction (Matt. 2:16). Jesus' disciples were outraged that a Samaritan village refused to receive Jesus. They wanted authority from Jesus to command fire to swoop down from heaven and incinerate the village (Luke 9:54).

If those hot-tempered Bible characters mentioned above had owned golf clubs, the air would have been thick with flying woods, irons, and putters.

The Bible counsels believers to get a grip on temper. It's okay to be angry about unrighteousness, inequity, injustice, and everything else that God despises; however, we must not let such anger drive us into sin. A believer would be justifiably angry because a neighbor beats his wife, but he would be wrong to vent that anger on his neighbor by beating him. Similarly, a believer should be angry if her employer engages in unethical business practices, but she would be wrong to retaliate by stealing from him. Also, a believer has the right to be angry about abortion, but he doesn't have the right to bomb an abortion clinic.

Read Proverbs 16:32 and Ephesians 4:26. List some things you are angry about. In each case, decide whether your anger is righteous or sinful, holy or hateful. Keep track of your temper's temperature. Don't let it approach the boiling point. Anger is just one letter short of danger.

14 ❑ A Courageous Player

Heather Farr, a native of Phoenix, Arizona, was emotionally and mentally tough, a strong competitor, and a true champion. Twice, she was all-American golfer at Arizona State. At age twenty, in 1986, she became the youngest player ever to qualify for the LPGA Tour. LPGA player Mary Bryan commented that when Heather first joined the tour "nobody worked harder. Heather was determined to do well. She was a very feisty young lady."

And Heather did well—very well! In three and a half years she won more than $170,000. Her future looked as bright as the Arizona sun. Then tragedy struck, and Heather faced a challenge much tougher than the LPGA Tour. She learned July 3, 1989, that she had breast cancer. Later that year, she reflected: "You go through life, especially as an athlete, thinking you're doing all the right things with your body. You never expect this to happen" (*The Chicago Tribune,* 20 November 1993).

In 1992 she said regarding cancer, "You play through it, that's what you do."

Until her death, November 20, 1993, Heather maintained a will-not-concede attitude in spite of fifteen operations, including a radical mastectomy, a bone marrow transplant, and spinal surgery. She was twenty-eight when she died.

In the same article quoted above, *The Chicago Tribune* reported that more than twenty pros demonstrating their respect and love for Heather were present at Scottsdale Memorial Hospital-North when she passed away.

The Bible acknowledges the uncertainty of life. We can't predict tomorrow's events. Nor can we know what will happen ten minutes from now. Whether sunshine or rain enters our lives, we need courage and faith to play the course God has laid out for us.

Life is too uncertain for any of us to be uncertain about living it the right way. Read James 1:1-5 and 4:14-17 today.

15 ❑ THE PROS' BIGGEST HANDICAP

W ouldn't it be great to be a resident golf pro at a private country club? After all, a pro gets paid to play golf. It doesn't get any better than that, you think. Well, you may want to take a closer look at the life of the resident golf pro.

I got my first good look at one golf pro's country-club life when I was fifteen years old. Known at the St. Catharines, Ontario, Golf Course, as a caddie and a junior golfer who had finished well in the Ontario Junior Golf Championship, I was hired to work summers for resident pro Alec Mackenzie. A Scotsman with a heavy brogue, Alec was highly regarded for his light touch on the greens and his delicate draws and fades.

Unfortunately for Alec, playing times were infrequent. Providing golf lessons and managing the pro shop, Alec was unable to do what he really wanted to do—play golf. Yet, the club members expected their pro to break par every time he hit the links.

Whenever Alec could leave the pro shop for a round of golf, he was like a fourth grader released for recess. Usually shy and a bit dour, Alex couldn't hide his excitement as tee time approached. His Scottish eyes brightened, a smile zipped across his face, and he talked incessantly.

Many resident golf pros today would be able to identify with Alec Mackenzie. Crushed with heavy administrative responsibilities, they find that their playing time has shrunk dramatically. Instead of being out on the course and improving their golf skills, they must supervise employees, maintain golf carts, instruct, sell equipment and merchandise, and handle the pro shop's finances.

Like many resident golf pros, pastors often get so loaded down with peripheral matters that they lack time for what counts most—prayer and the study and preaching of God's Word. Consider how you might be able to help reduce the load of peripheral responsibilities that rests on your pastor's shoulders. Tell your pastor you want to help. Share your ideas with him, and be open to any suggestions he may offer. Your concern might spread to others and, as a result, transform your pastor into a facsimile of a fourth grader released for recess or an Alec MacKenzie striding full speed ahead to the first tee.

Read Acts 6:1-7 and 1 Thessalonians 5:12-13. Pray for your pastor, and guard your time of fellowship with God. As someone has cautioned, "Beware of the barrenness of a busy life."

16 ❑ GOLF: THE CHOICE of CHAMPIONS

Michael Jordan. The name is synonymous with basketball greatness. Famous for his spectacular moves, drives to the hoop, and last-second, game-winning shots, Michael led the Chicago Bulls to three NBA Championships. Then surprisingly, in 1993, he announced his retirement from basketball. Soon, he appeared in a Chevrolet commercial. The commercial showed MJ packing his golf clubs into a Chevy Blazer. A bluebird perched on a branch, framed against a blue sky, catches Michael's eye just before he drives away to enjoy a day of golf. Probably, since its first showing, the commercial has attracted at least as many people to golf as it has to Chevrolet.

Now Michael's back in the NBA and in new TV commercials, but I don't think many fans will forget the Blazer episode.

Golf seems to be the common denominator for athletes from many sports. Who hasn't seen TV footage of football players and coaches driving or putting in some charity golf tournament? When I caddied in my early teen years in Canada, I occasionally carried clubs for members of the Toronto Maple Leafs. Sometimes, I played golf with members of my hometown's Junior OHA hockey team, the St. Catharines Teepees. My biggest thrill, though, was to caddie one day in 1950 for world heavyweight champion Joe Louis.

Retired from boxing, Joe had come to St. Catharines for a personal appearance. I learned from caddying for him that he hadn't left his power in the ring. He could punch a golf ball three hundred yards off the tee. He was almost as accurate in landing a shot on the green as he had been in landing a right cross to the jaw.

Joe Louis was a gentleman on the course. Soft-spoken and friendly, he took time to talk to me as we walked each fairway. He even paused along the way to let someone take a picture of him and me together. Hanging in my office, that photo rekindles a cherished memory of the day I caddied for the world heavyweight boxing champion.

Just as golf provides a common ground for athletes from many sports, so Christianity provides a common ground for believers from all walks of life. In Christ we are one. Whether we are African-American, Hispanic, Asian, Native American, European, or Anglo, male or female, we are one body. Neither fame nor obscurity, wealth nor poverty, much education nor little education, high social standing nor low social standing can destroy the reality of our oneness in Christ.

———

Read Jesus' prayer for all believers in John 17, then thank your heavenly Father for the common ground you and your Christian brothers and sisters have in Christ. Extend the circle of your friendship to other believers, and talk about the good life you share in Christ.

17 ❑ THE MAKER LEFT HIS MARK

In 1991 I started collecting old golf clubs—the hand-forged, wood-shafted kind that predate 1935, the year I was born. I cut my golf teeth on wood-shafted clubs, so I feel kind of sentimental about my hobby. Finding such a club at a flea market or garage sale is like discovering a lost relative.

Before 1890 blacksmiths made clubheads by heating iron bars in forges and then pounding them into shape by hand. By the turn of the century steam-powered hammers lightened the work, but the manufacturing process still required patience and skill. The British iron makers in the 1880s-1920s era became known as cleek makers, and stamped their identifying mark, called a "cleek mark," on their clubheads.

I doubt that anyone today would try to make a living by making clubs the old-fashioned way. He would go broke faster than a new golf ball goes out of bounds. Nevertheless, the old-time club makers managed to put bread on the table and pride into their work. Their cleek marks represent their good name.

Many collectors try to obtain clubs having different cleek marks, and the fun of doing so is as endless as the range of cleek marks seems to be. A shepherd's crook identifies Alex Shepherd as a club maker around 1915. Alex Patrick put the spur mark on his work between 1905 and 1915. Andrew Herd Scott, club maker for England's George V, used a crown and lion from 1911 to 1925. St. Andrew Golf Company used the stag mark from 1910 until 1925 and introduced a sun mark in 1925. Gene Sarazen used St. Andrew clubs in the 1930s.

The list of cleeks could go on, but I will mention only a few more: a pipe, a serpent, a robin, a flag, an anchor, an anvil, a hammer, a bear, a thistle, and a Scottish bluebell.

Ephesians 2:10 indicates that every Christian is a product of God's workmanship. We were like scrap iron before He reached down to salvage us. When He put His hands on us, He purged us of our sin and began to forge and polish us into the image of His Son (Rom. 8:29). Someday, the forging and polishing will end, and we will be like Christ (1 John 3:2). However, God has already stamped His "cleek mark" on each of us. According to Ephesians 1:13, God has sealed us with the Holy Spirit. This "seal" guarantees that God will perfect His work in us.

A cleek mark on an antique golf club enables its owner to identify the maker and admire his work. The Holy Spirit's presence in your life identifies you as a product of God's grace and proves that He is forging and polishing you into the image of His Son. Thank Him for His grace, love, and patience. Glorify Him as your Maker and Redeemer. Read Ephesians 2:1-10.

18 ❑ Golf's Grand Slam Champion

When it comes to golf's greatest champions, the name of Bobby Jones comes to mind. A legend whose name is linked forever with the Masters tournament, Bobby Jones won golf's four most prestigious tournaments the same year. He was only twenty-eight in 1930 when he swept both the Open and Amateur championships in America and Britain. And he did it all with hickory-shafted clubs!

Winning those four tournaments in the same year is called the Grand Slam or The Impregnable Quadrilateral, and it is considered the most perfect accomplishment in golf.

Jones got an early start toward winning the Grand Slam.

Bobby's family had moved into an Atlanta neighborhood, across from the East Lake Club, when he was a young boy. Being so close to East Lake, Bobby could see golfers in action. However, his father wasn't interested in golf, so his mother took him to East Lake, where at age five he swung a golf club for the first time.

Under the watchful eye of East Lake's pro, Bobby developed into an outstanding young golfer. At nine he won the junior championship of the East Lake Club. At fourteen he snatched up the Georgia State Amateur championship. When he was only eighteen, he finished eighth in the U.S. Open. By the time he was twenty-eight, he had captured thirteen national championships between 1923 and 1930.

What golfer hasn't watched the Masters tournament on TV and

been impressed with the beauty of the host course, Augusta National? Bobby Jones guided the building of Augusta National, and he was the inspiration behind the Masters tournament.

In later life, Jones faced his toughest opponent, a crippling disease that confined him to a wheelchair and eventually took his life. He died in December, 1971, at age sixty-nine. Later, a friend of Bobby Jones commented that forbearance in his battle with the disease had been his greatest triumph.

The Bible doesn't mention a Grand Slam championship, but it does mention four crowns: the "crown of rejoicing" (1 Thess. 2:19), "the crown of righteousness" (2 Tim. 4:8), "the crown of life" (James 1:12), and "the crown of glory" (1 Peter 5:4). In golf only one outstanding player can win the Grand Slam; but in Christian living every faithful believer can win all four crowns.

When Bobby Jones closed in on the last green in the final tournament in the Grand Slam, he must have felt exhilarated. If he could just win that last hole, he would receive the trophy that would crown his finest year of golf and immortalize him as the Grand Slam champion. The faithful Christian ought to feel exhilarated, too, because soon he or she will see Jesus. "I am coming quickly," He promised, "and My reward is with Me" (Rev. 22:12).

Who knows, today we may reach the final green!

Course Number 2:
Desert Springs

I will open rivers in desolate heights,
And fountains in the midst of the valleys;
I will make the wilderness a pool of water,
And the dry land springs of water.
Isaiah 41:18

1 ❑ HOLE in ONE on the TOLLWAY!

A justifiably angry motorist would like to find the golfer who scored a hole in one on the Tri-State, the tollway that skirts Chicago and links Illinois to northwest Indiana and southeast Wisconsin.

The motorist was sitting in snarled traffic on the Tri-State when a golf ball rocketed from a local golf course and smashed through his car's passenger-side window. Somebody had scored a tollway hole in one, but the motorist wasn't about to celebrate the accomplishment.

Believing that the course should be held liable for damages, the motorist drove to the course and reported what had happened. However, the business manager informed him that the "shooter" was solely responsible.

So, if the complainant wants someone to pay for the damages to his car, he will have to identify the golfer and establish his guilt. In the meantime, he is urging the state to require safety nets where fairways run alongside major roads.

The ace tollway golfer wasn't the first or the last player to hit into traffic, and he may not have seen where his ball landed. If he reacted as I suspect he did, he probably covered his ears, closed his eyes, and hoped for the best when he saw his tee shot zoom toward the tollway. Given an opportunity to vote on a safety-net referendum, he and every bound-to-be-wild golfer would vote yes. No one in his right mind wants to damage property or injure a motorist. He might even be willing to pay a slightly higher greens fee to cover the cost of installing the nets.

Like golf shots, words cannot be called back. And, like golf balls landing in traffic, words carry the potential to injure and even to kill. Who hasn't felt wounded by malicious gossip or unjust criticism? And who can't identify at least one good reputation that was killed by deadly rumors and innuendos?

How can we Christians protect ourselves and others from injurious verbal shots? Obviously we can't drape safety nets over people's mouths, but we can campaign for wholesome, kind, and gracious speech by setting the right example. We can ask the Lord to post a guard over our mouths and lips (Ps. 141:3) and then steer well-chosen words in the right direction.

Read James 3 today for a penetrating, accurate description of the power of words. Words can edify or destroy, help or hurt, soothe or sting. In each conversation today, select your words carefully. Then send them prayerfully on their way to encourage and to comfort.

2 ❑ GOLF B.C.—BEFORE CARTS

I don't know when golf carts first rolled down Canadian fairways. If they were available to Canadian golfers before the early 1950s, they must have appeared only rarely as UFOs (Unusual Fairway Objects). I caddied at a private Canadian course from 1942 to 1951 and then worked in the pro shop for a couple of years, but I didn't see a golf cart in all that time.

Of course, caddies were more plentiful in golf's B.C. (before carts) history. On any given summer day, the caddie shack was full of youngsters who were eager to lug golf bags for less than a dollar. Most of us caddies—boys and girls—came from a poor- to modest-income neighborhood that formed the course's northern border.

Pulling a cart or riding in a cart may spare a golfer's strength, but a good caddie might save his game. Caddying meant far more to us caddies than simply carrying a bag of clubs or locating balls or tending flags; it also meant recommending the right clubs for the right shots and showing loyalty and propriety at all times. Tremendous responsibilities for anyone earning less than a dollar!

I think I was a good caddie. Even when a narrow bag strap cut into my shoulder, I didn't flinch. I located many an out-of-bounds or in-the-rough ball, recommended the right club in most situations, tended flags with military precision, and displayed loyalty akin to that of a president's bodyguard. However, at times a sense of humor endangered my reputation. The sight of a golfer's divot sailing farther than his ball would send such waves of glee crashing against my liver that I couldn't hide a smile or choke back a chuckle.

I bit holes into my tongue so many times that it's a wonder I can talk without whistling.

Perhaps the best thing about pre-cart golf was the heritage golfers passed on to their caddies. The good golfers taught us what to do, and the hackers showed us what to avoid. Caddying, then, afforded me and others like me the opportunity to learn golf without having to pay for lessons.

Christian culture has attained a high degree of sophistication. Today, experts teach seminars in marriage, family living, successful singleness, confidence building, evangelism, personal finances, Christian education, creativity, music, and prayer. Why, there are so many seminars that it's possible to overspend and overdose on them. And although many of them are helpful, they are no substitute for personal, daily discipleship. Every wise seminar instructor will attest to the incomparable value packed into a mentor-disciple relationship. As growing Christians see Christianity fleshed out in the life of mature believers, they learn how to play the game of life. And the lessons are free!

Discipleship is basic to vital Christianity. Jesus instructed His followers to carry the good news of salvation to all nations and to disciple those who believed (Matt. 28:19-20). From then until now, the best disciplers have also been the best disciples. Those who strive to know Christ better are also those who portray Him best. Read and appropriate 1 Timothy 4:12-16 today. Someone wants to learn from your example.

3 ❑ DRIVING-RANGE BLUES

D etermined to add distance and accuracy to their game, golfers are turning to driving ranges in record numbers. Weekend warriors and veterans of fairway wars join forces along a line of rubber mats to fire off golf balls by the bucketload. Yardage markers serve as targets at most driving ranges; however, rough-hewn greens are targets at other ranges.

If you visit a driving range, you will find that it doesn't make any difference what targets lie in front of the warriors. When they miss badly, the frustration shows. Sometimes it slips out in verbal language. At other times it shows in body language such as hands on the hips for a whiff, a low forward bend and an extended club for a topped ball, a slap to the forehead for a banana drive, or two steps back for a worm burner.

So, move over, New Orleans, driving ranges everywhere are becoming famous for the blues!

But there is a ray of hope. Practice, practice, and more practice can chase the blues away and usher in the sweet sounds of well-hit shots on a golf course. Show me a par shooter, and I'll show you a golfer who refused to let discouragement defeat him.

Is there a Christian anywhere who hasn't sung the blues?

Of course not. Every Christian gets discouraged at one time or another. We have all experienced our share of missed targets, embarrassing slipups, and failure, but we don't have to surrender to discouragement. By faith we can put the worst behind us and press on to the best—consistent victory.

In the eighth century B.C., Ahaz, King of Judah, faced a double threat. The king of Israel and the king of Syria had joined forces against him. What was Ahaz to do? Cower in fear? Buckle under to discouragement and then surrender to the enemy? He could have given up, but he didn't because the prophet Isaiah brought him an encouraging message from the Lord. "Take heed, and be quiet; do not fear or be fainthearted" (Isa. 7:4), the Lord counseled Ahaz. The Lord would defeat the enemy's plans (vv. 5-7).

For a personalized message of encouragement from the Lord, read Philippians 4:6-7.

4 ☐ SHAGGING BALLS

T hink about it. If fifty golfers respectively hit fifty range balls in a given thirty-minute period, how many balls would litter a driving range in a day if they were not retrieved? Understanding the logistics of this situation, driving ranges have devised a way to bring their range balls home to their buckets. Tractors, equipped to scoop the balls from the ground, roam the range. Like armored tanks under fire, they roll along, impervious to missiles and determined to accomplish their mission.

If you have watched members of the driving-range armored division do their job, you have observed at least two absolutes: (1) every tractor cab is surrounded with a steel-mesh cage, and (2) the biggest harvest of range balls comes from an area between the 50-yard and 150-yard markers. The picking gets slimmer as the yardage increases.

I wonder how long a range-ball retriever must work to become calm under fire. Do some retrievers suffer shell shock and look for some other line of work? I wonder how many of those tractor drivers would be willing to stand in the open range, unprotected and charged with the task of retrieving range balls for thirty cents per hour? None. (Well, one might consent to do so after getting struck on the head by a line drive.)

Nevertheless, about fifty years ago many caddies received about thirty cents per hour to shag balls. The job required a caddie to stand as a target in the bull pen (driving range), retrieve each ball driven at him, and place it into a canvas bag about the size of a lady's medium-size handbag. A wave of a golfer's hand would signal the caddie to stand closer to him or farther away. When a golfer had expended his supply of balls, the caddie would run to him and empty the canvas bag at his feet. Then golfer and caddie would repeat the process until the golfer called it quits.

Shagging balls lofted by a nine iron was a snap. The mid-iron shots presented a greater challenge. But the two-iron and three-iron shots were almost murder, especially at the hands of an accurate golfer framed by a glaring sun. Caddies considered it macho to catch a line drive in the canvas bag, but a miss often meant getting hit on a wrist, a leg, or a side. I know. After getting hit, I wore a ball-logo impression for days as a badge of courage (or stupidity).

Shagging balls might be considered a severe form of child abuse today. For me as a kid, it was a way to earn money. I often wonder, though, was it worth the risk? I could have been killed.

I like to think my philosophy of life has matured since ball-shagging days. I believe money isn't as important as so many treadmill-bound, materialistic men and women make it out to be. A refrigerator magnet in my daughter Sherrie and son-in-law Jim's home puts it all into perspective. "The best things in life aren't things," it affirms.

Redeemed people are the objects of divine care and the recipients of a high calling. If all the money and possessions in the world were stacked together, they would fall far short of the level of life God has designated for us. He has raised us up to sit with Christ in the heavenlies and to enjoy some of heaven's treasures even now. Read Colossians 3:1-3 today. Don't risk losing what God considers truly valuable to gain what He considers of little worth.

5 ❑ THE GOLF-BALL NOSE TEST

What do you look for in a golf ball? High trajectory? Low trajectory? Tough cover? Long distance? Although personal preferences vary, every golfer wants to hit a ball that has lots of life. You know, one that takes off like a Polaris missile upon impact. But it seems that you have to be an aerospace engineer or some kind of physics expert to figure out the right ball to use for specific golfing conditions.

When I was a boy, selecting the best golf ball was a simple task. It was just a matter of applying a quick, no-cost test to any ball in question. If I had to name the test today, I would call it the golf-ball nose test. Here's how it worked.

A golfer would select two golf balls at a time and carry them to a sidewalk or cement driveway. Then he would stand erect, holding both balls at the tip of his nose. He would release them together and would observe which ball bounced higher. The higher the bounce, the more life to the ounce! An average bounce reached the belt line. A particularly lively ball might reach the chest. Any golf ball that failed to reach the belt line was considered "dead." Those that had been fished out of a water hazard after a lengthy aquatic stay were almost always dead. After subjecting all their golf balls to the nose test, golfers would choose the liveliest ones with absolute confidence.

Believers and unbelievers are alike in many ways. Both experience happiness and sadness, good days and rough days, wellness and illness, and numerous other life episodes. However, believers and unbelievers respond differently under testing. When adversity strikes unbelievers, they are likely to fall flat and then experience a slow and painful recovery. They lack resilience because they lack spiritual life. Believers, on the other hand, bounce back from adversity—vigorously and energetically. When tested, they show by their faith that they are spiritually alive. And not surprisingly, God chooses to use in significant ways those who bounce back the highest.

Consider what Job endured by faith. Tested severely and repeatedly, he demonstrated unshakable confidence in God's wisdom and fairness. He confessed: "Though He slay me, yet will I trust Him" (Job 13:15). If you want to see how far Job bounced back when tested, read Job 42:10-13. Meet each test—big or small—with faith. It will put more bounce in your walk with God.

6 ❑ BD GOL4

S tated at one time or another by nearly every underachieving golfer after recording an embarrassingly high score: "Does anyone want the scorecard? If nobody wants it, I'll tear it up and toss it in the trash can."

Stated at one time or another by nearly every overachieving golfer after recording his all-time best score: "If it's okay with everybody, I'd like to keep the scorecard. I want to frame it and hang it on a wall at home."

That's the way it is with golf and golfers. Who wants to advertise a failure? Who doesn't want to perpetuate the memory of a personal best?

Surprisingly, I recently saw a "vanity" license plate announcing BD GOL4. Apparently the motorist is determined to tell the whole driving public that he is a bad golfer.

It is remotely possible that BD stands for "Birdie," but wouldn't a birdie golfer be sure to include an R between B and D?

I'm quite sure BD GOL4 means "Bad Golfer." Perhaps the motorist believes strongly in public confession. Perhaps he was compelled by an off-the-wall sense of humor to select the vanity license plate. At any rate, I applaud his transparent honesty and/or his ability to laugh at himself.

If believers followed BD GOL4's example and publicized their personal weaknesses or bad habits on vanity license plates, would the following messages flow through traffic?

LA Z	CUSR
LI OF10	O4 ETR
PAY L8	EGO 1
RIPUOFF	HOT HEAD
CHEAT 2	GOLDIGR

Fortunately, God has provided a much better way for believers to deal with bad habits and besetting sins. He urges us to confess them, lay them aside like worn-out clothes, and replace them with Christlike virtues.

Read 1 John 1:9 and Colossians 3:8-14. If you need victory over a nagging bad habit, claim that victory now. Who knows, you may want to celebrate by purchasing a license plate that reads 4GVN or PSM 103 12.

7 ❑ SNAKE in the GRASS

Some people get along just fine with snakes. I've seen snake owners drape boas and assorted other slithery creatures around their necks and wear them with pride. To each his own, I guess, but just the thought of having a snake for a pet sends icy chills down my spine.

Once, a snake kept me awake all night. I was a family's guest at the time and was scheduled to preach at their church the following morning. They had given me their teenage son's bedroom, complete with dresser, chair, a narrow bed—and a huge snake they called Tarzan.

Tarzan was housed in a glass aquarium not more than ten inches from the head of the bed. A screen served as the aquarium's lid. A heavy rock rested on the screen to keep Tarzan in his territory.

I didn't sleep that night. Somehow, I kept one eye open and focused on Tarzan. He spent the night slithering up the aquarium walls and bumping his head on the screen. Escape must have been in his game plan, perhaps to get better acquainted with me.

Getting cozy with a snake is not my idea of a fun time.

Apparently, it isn't U.S. Open champion Ernie Els's idea of a fun time either. The South African Press Association reported that Els encountered a poisonous snake while playing in the Nashua Wild Coast Challenge.

Els shrugged off his encounter with the three-foot adder that exited a patch of long grass off the sixteenth hole and then wiggled toward him. But judge for yourself whether it affected his game.

Shortly after eluding the adder, the South African ace placed a wedge shot into a pond. It cost him a bogey on the sixteenth hole. Then, a bad drive on the seventeenth led to a double bogey. He closed out five strokes shy of the winner Hendrik Buhrmann.

The believer's worst enemy is the devil. Revelation 12:9 identifies him as "that serpent of old" and charges him with the crime of deceiving the whole world. Like a snake in the grass, the devil often shows up when and where he is least expected. He may appear in an attractive business deal, in a "harmless" social relationship, or in a new and intriguing religious teaching. Then he strikes furiously, spewing deadly venom and ruining what seemed like a good day—even a good life. The believer must stay alert to the devil, knowing his modus operandi. And he must resist him in the faith (1 Pet. 5:9). Otherwise, he will experience defeat—possibly, major defeat.

Read Genesis 3:1-9 and 1 Peter 5:8-9. Be cautious today. The serpent's hiss is in every ssssin. Watch and pray!

8 ❏ JOE KIRKWOOD: TRICK-SHOT ARTIST

K eep your head down and your eye on the ball. Excellent advice! But Joe Kirkwood proved he could hit beautiful shots with his head up and his eyes focused on his admiring fans.

I saw him do it in 1951, when he performed a trick-shot show at my home course. I had seen his movie-star son act in the role of cartoon boxer Joe Palooka. His punches were dynamite! Dad Kirkwood demonstrated dynamite punches too. After teeing up six or seven balls in a straight line, he punched them, one after the other in rapid succession, sending all of them about 275 yards down the middle of the fairway. And he did it with his head up and his eyes trained on the spectators.

Joe demonstrated, too, that he could choose to slice, hook, or hit a straight shot. After lining up three balls, he drove them down the fairway. The first went straight. The second sliced over the path of the first shot. The third hooked over the path of the first.

After stomping a ball into the ground, he hit a perfect wood shot. After teeing another ball about two feet off the ground, he drove it far and straight.

An extremely long driver with an enormous head and another with a ropelike flexible shaft were just two of the goofy clubs Joe Kirkwood used to entertain the crowd.

I was able to learn one trick from Joe's repertoire. He placed one ball on top of another. Then he hit the bottom ball straight out, sending the top ball about ten feet straight up. Then he caught the top ball in his hand as it descended. I like to perform that stunt for anybody who'll watch.

Unfortunately, I failed to learn a more delicate Joe Kirkwood trick. The trick called for a volunteer to lie down on his back. Joe placed a wad of chewing gum on the toe of the volunteer's right shoe, set a golf ball on the gum, and then teed off. The volunteer suffered no harm, and the shoe was unmarred. A few days after the Joe Kirkwood performance, I persuaded a friend to let me tee off from his foot. It would be my first attempt at duplicating Joe Kirkwood's shoe shot. It would also be my last attempt. A large leather divot proved I was no Joe Kirkwood! Some things are better left to the experts.

Christian living, too, is better left to the expert, Jesus Christ. If we try to perform spiritual deeds by our own ability, we will fail. We may even cause damage far more severe than the leather divot caused by my ill-famed shoe shot. Without Jesus Christ, we can do nothing (John 15:5). But through Him, we can do "all things" (Phil. 4:13).

Think about it: If an expert golf pro could step into your golf shoes and hit every shot for you, would he significantly improve your game? You know he would. Christ lives in you, and He wants to live through you. Trust Him to do just that, and watch Him improve your living skills significantly. Trust, not tricks, is the way to play the game of life. Read John 15:1-5 and Galatians 2:20 today.

9 ❑ FAVORITE CLUB

It's the club you feel most comfortable with. It gives you confidence. It has pulled you out of tight spots before; it will do it again. It's your favorite club. No, you don't sleep with it, but you might not sleep very well if you lost it or broke it.

My favorite club is the six iron. I was nine years old when I purchased my first club, a Spalding Robert T. Jones six iron. It cost about five dollars, roughly the amount of money I had earned from caddying 125 holes. It took a lot of work to obtain that six iron, but it was more than worth the effort.

While saving for a second club, I gave the Bobby Jones six iron quite a workout. I found that I could drive with it by closing the face of the club and taking a long grip. For short-iron shots, I opened the face, took a short grip and short swing.

In sand traps around greens, my six iron became a sand wedge. I laid the clubhead as far back as possible and used a flat swing to blast out and land softly on the carpet.

To this day, my best chip shots have been six iron chips.

Occasionally one drops in from the fringe and makes me profoundly happy that I invested five dollars a long time ago.

Evangelist and Bible teacher Vance Havner used to tell his audiences, "God doesn't have favorites, but He does have intimates." He understood that God "shows no partiality" (Acts 10:34) but that He does cultivate close friendships. He wants His children to draw close to Him (James 4:8), to talk freely and openly with Him (Phil. 4:6; Heb. 4:16), and to get to know Him well (Col. 1:10).

Abraham was one of God's intimates; James 2:23 calls him "the friend of God." When his love for God was tested, Abraham showed that his love for God exceeded even his love for his son Isaac (Gen. 22:1-19).

And there was Job. God called him "My servant Job," adding that Job was in a class by himself, "a blameless and upright man, one who fears God and shuns evil" (Job 1:8).

Moses was another of God's intimates. He and God had private conversations in Midian (Ex. 3-4), on Mount Sinai (chapters 19-40), and at the close of Moses' life, on Mount Nebo (Deut. 34:1-6).

David, too, enjoyed an intimate relationship with God. God identified him as "a man after My own heart" (Acts 13:22).

A list of God's intimates would surely include Peter, James, and John, the inner circle of Jesus' disciples. Also, the apostle Paul would make the list. Between his conversion and the beginning of his public ministry, Paul spent more than three years alone with God in the Arabian desert (Gal. 1:15-24).

The believer's work for God is important, but his or her walk with God is crucial. Read Micah 6:8 and Philippians 3:8-10 today. Time spent with God is far more valuable than time spent any other way—even time spent with your favorite golf club!

10 ❑ GOLF WORLD'S EIGHTEEN-YEAR-OLD MAN of the YEAR

An eighteen-year-old outstanding athlete might have difficulty choosing a college education over the highly lucrative life of a professional athlete, but at age eighteen Eldrick "Tiger" Woods opted for student life at Stanford University.

Tiger entered Stanford in 1994 with the U.S. Amateur championship in his hand. At eighteen he was its youngest champion. Jack Nicklaus was nineteen when he won the championship. Also to his credit, in 1994 Tiger was named Man of the Year by *Golf World.*

It would likely be hard for Tiger Woods to recall a time when he didn't play golf. He shot 48 for nine holes when he was just three.

In his freshman year Tiger was held up on campus at knife point. His assailant robbed him of a watch and gold chain, and then slugged him in the jaw. Nevertheless, Tiger remained determined to stay on at Stanford and complete his studies. He is a promising young golfer with a strong grip on correct priorities.

A young Pharisee in New Testament times faced a crossroads decision. Known as Saul of Tarsus, he had stood head and shoulders above his classmates in rabbinical seminary. He would have won any vote to be the student most likely to succeed. He had a rich Hebrew culture, held membership in the tribe of Benjamin—the tribe that had given Israel her first king and had stood alongside the tribe of Judah when the other tribes revolted and formed their own kingdom. He bore the name of Israel's first king, and he was unrivaled for devotion to Israel's law and traditions. Then, on the road to Damascus, Saul encountered the risen Christ, and his life and priorities changed as he bowed to Christ's authority. His former, selfish priorities vanished; knowing and serving Christ became his top priorities. And he never wavered from them. He closed the final chapter of his life, having fulfilled God's will and anticipating God's reward.

Someone advised, "Don't sacrifice the future on the altar of the immediate." Keeping our priorities in line with God's will makes the present worthwhile and the future glorious. Read Acts 26:1-23 today.

11 ❑ Cancer Recovery, Course Record

P aul Azinger is an amazing person with a captivating smile. In 1993 he had good reason to smile; he was the year's PGA champion. That same year, though, he must have found it hard to smile. Diagnosed with lymphoma, a form of cancer, this bright, young golf pro looked at an uncertain future. Would his bout with cancer damage his career? Would he lose the opportunity to be competitive in major tournaments? The disease in his left shoulder would challenge his body and his spirit.

Emerging from his battle with cancer, Paul Azinger missed the cut in the Buick Open and the PGA Championship. The Buick Southern Open and the Walt Disney Classic were more to his liking, but he didn't unseat the leaders.

But December 17, 1994, Azinger proved that he was back in the hunt. Playing the Tyrall Course, he posted a nine-under-par 62, a course record. The previous record 63 was posted by Greg Norman.

The golfer who attributes a high score to his clogged sinuses or cold sores needs to reflect on Paul Azinger's indomitable spirit.

First Kings 19 uncovers the sad story that Elijah was as downcast as anyone can get. Deep in the stark and forlorn wilderness south of Judah, he sat alone and wailed about God's unfairness and about how rotten life had become. After all, that bloodthirsty prophet-hater, Jezebel, had put a contract out on his life. He felt hopeless, helpless, and horrid. He wondered why God didn't just end his life there in the wilderness. Then patiently and tenderly, God drew Elijah's attention away from his awful situation to God's all-sufficiency. He showed Elijah that the believer's life is in His hands. He revealed that Elijah's ministry wasn't over; He had special assignments for Elijah.

The believer who looks at circumstances may see defeat, but the believer who looks at God's all-sufficiency sees every day as a day of unparalleled potential.

Read Numbers 13:17-14:10. Dare to trust God for victory over giant obstacles. Refuse to succumb to self-pity. Recognize that even the bleakest day can end as the brightest day because the Ancient of Days is in control of your life.

12 ❑ THE CASE of the GOLF-BUDDY BURGLAR

I passed through Kewanee, Illinois, at Christmastime in 1994. Its Christmas lights and decorations projected good cheer and charm. It appeared to be a typical Midwestern neighborly kind of town. But Kewanee had just discovered that one of its "friendly" neighbors was actually a rogue, a perpetrator of eighty-five burglaries.

Prior to his arrest, the accused burglar's reputation seemed to be 100 percent pure—squeaky clean. He taught Sunday school, dropped in on neighbors for friendly chats, invited folks to lunch, and was golf buddy to a number of local golfers. He was the kind of citizen any town would be proud of. However, "Mr. Friendly's" reputation was simply a put-on, a smoke screen that allowed him ready access to Kewanee houses.

During each of his neighborly visits, the Sunday school teacher/burglar would gather crucial information about the location of valuables. At neighborly lunches he would excuse himself, hurry to his lunch partner's home, burglarize it, and hurry back to finish lunch.

The Kewanee burglar's golf friends fared no better than his other victims. He would arrange to play golf with a friend but would arrive late for the tee time. While his friend waited patiently for him, the good-old-golf-buddy burglar would be rummaging through his friend's home and carting off his valuables.

A golf buddy who cheats on the course violates *The Rules of Golf,* but a golf buddy who burglarizes his golfing friend's home violates the rules of civility. His crime is downright indecent, despicable, and abhorrent.

Fortunately the golf-buddy burglar got what he deserved.

He was apprehended as he exited a house. Police caught him red-handed; he was carrying off a loot of valuable coins. Now Kewanee can get back to the business of trusting its friendly citizens to be genuinely friendly. And golfers don't have to hire detectives to check into their golf buddies' backgrounds. They may even tee it up on time!

One of Jesus' disciples pretended to be a friend. Judas Iscariot traveled with Jesus, listened to His parables and sermons, and ate with Him. Who would have guessed that Judas the disciple was friendly only for a selfish purpose? He wanted to cash in on the success he thought lay ahead in Jesus' kingdom. When his dream of becoming rich vanished, he betrayed Jesus for thirty pieces of silver.

Unlike the Kewanee golfers who were deceived by their golf buddy, Jesus was not fooled by Judas's feigned friendship. "One of you will betray Me," Jesus told His disciples at the Last Supper (John 13:21). Even when Judas later kissed Jesus in the Garden of Gethsemane, Jesus knew that it was a kiss of betrayal. He has always been able to distinguish His true friends from those who simply want to get something from Him.

Friendship is a sacred trust. Friends help one another, support one another, and serve one another. Evaluate your friendship with Jesus Christ and others in the light of John 15:14 and Proverbs 17:17.

13 ❑ SLOW FOURSOME AHEAD

Likely, more Christians have had their sanctification sorely tested by a slow foursome in front of them than by natural hazards—including wide ponds, hidden creeks, and deep ravines. It just isn't spiritually invigorating to address a ball and at the same time see a couple of golfers emerge from a wooded area less than two hundred yards ahead and then see two more pop up out of a bunker. That's enough grief to cause even a preacher to think about praying for permission to call down fire from heaven on four heads!

And why do the slowest, worst golfers on the course spend the longest time on each green? It seems that it takes them longer to read each green than it would for a beginning English student to read an entire set of *Encyclopaedia Britannica*. When they finally get into a putting stance, they stand motionless for what seems like an eternity.

Well, there are some ways to cope with the slow-foursome syndrome. Here's what you can do when you can't play through:

- Lie down. Stretch out on soft, green fairway grass. Breathe deeply. Gaze at God's vast, blue sky. Relax, and marvel at God's creative power.
- Practice your swing, aiming away from the slow foursome. Now is an opportune time to work on slowing your backswing.
- Determine not to rush your next shot.
- Compile a mental list of ten reasons to be thankful.

- Meditate on a familiar passage of Scripture.
- Pray for your pastor. At that moment he may be facing a far more stressful situation than you are.
- Track your way through a log of memorized Scripture verses.
- Contemplate what really matters most in life.

The Bible sometimes tunes us in to what we would rather not hear. Romans 5:3 presents one of those occasions, informing us that tribulation develops patience. An illness, a job layoff, a leaky roof, and a scrunched car are just a few of the tribulations that build patience into our lives. At first they may be more unwelcome than a slow foursome, but eventually we discover that God has used those tribulations to slow us down and cause us to communicate with Him.

Job never played golf behind a slow foursome, but he contended with excruciatingly painful calamities and extremely insensitive "friends." Nevertheless, he remained patient, and the Lord rewarded his patience (James 5:11). Read James 5:7-11 and practice the patience of Job—off the course and on it too.

14 ◻ OUTSTANDING WOMEN GOLFERS (1940s-70s)

G olf has given the sports world some tremendous female athletes. Here are just a few of the many who have contributed so much to the advancement and excitement of women's golf.

Babe Didrikson Zaharias

This remarkable 1932 Olympics champion turned her attention to golf in 1935. Her credits include fifty-five pro and amateur wins and ten majors, three of which were U.S. Women's Opens (1948, '50, '54). She also poured her energies into the founding of the LPGA in 1949. The following year she was named Female Athlete of the Half Century by the Associated Press.

Patty Berg

Acclaimed AP Female Athlete of the Year in 1938, '43, and '55, Patty racked up fifty-seven career pro wins, including fifteen majors. She won the U.S. Women's Open in 1946. Among other accomplishments, she helped to found the LPGA and served as its first president for four years.

Betsy Rawls

Betsy won the U.S. Women's Open four times (1951, '53, '57, '60) and also achieved two LPGA Championships (1959, '69).

Mickey Wright

This talented golfer put four U.S. Women's Open Championships in her pocket (1958, '59, '61, '64) and found additional space there for four LPGA Championships (1958, '60, '61, '63) and one Colgate Dinah Shore Championship (1973). Her career tallied eighty-two wins including thirteen majors.

Kathy Whitworth

If seven represents perfection, as many Bible teachers claim, Kathy Whitworth must have played perfect golf in the 1960s and '70s. Seven times she was LPGA Player of the Year (1966-69,71-73). She won LPGA Championships in 1967, '71, and '75 as well as the Colgate Dinah Shore Championship in 1977.

The church owes a debt of gratitude to women. So many of them have done so much for the cause of Christ that only heaven's record books can hold all their names and accomplishments. The New Testament annals of church history include names of many women who performed extraordinary ministry.

Read Matthew 27:55-56 as well as 28:10. Devout women were loyal followers of Christ in Galilee. They did not abandon Him when He was dying. And they were the first to visit His tomb and to hail His resurrection. Today, too, devout women follow and serve Christ. Even a casual glance at your church's missionary bulletin board or list of Christian workers will show how much your church depends on your sisters in Christ. As you pray today, include a word of thanks for women who love the Lord.

15 ❑ OUTSTANDING WOMEN GOLFERS (1980s-90s)

Every new decade ushers in another class of outstanding women golfers. Here are a few who made women's golf in the 1980s and '90s so memorable.

Nancy Lopez

Introduced to golf by her father, Nancy took to golf like a kid takes to ice cream. At age twelve, she won the New Mexico Women's Amateur. It would be the first in a long string of championships, including nine Tour events in 1978, including the LPGA Championship. She was 1978 Rookie of the Year and Player of the Year in 1978, 1979, 1985, and 1988. She captured the Nabisco Dinah Shore Championship in 1981 and LPGA Championships again in 1985 and 1989. In the 1985 LPGA Championship she set a new LPGA record for scoring average of 70.73. She was inducted into the LPGA Hall of Fame in 1987 after winning her thirty-fifth official tournament, the Sarasota Classic.

Patty Sheehan

Rookie of the Year in 1981, Patty Sheehan had already won numerous amateur events, including the Nevada State Amateur from 1975 through 1978 and the California Amateur in 1978 and 1979. She racked up twenty-five victories in her first ten full years on the LPGA Tour, including two majors, the 1983 and 1984 LPGA Championships. She placed second three times in the U.S. Women's Open (1983, '88, and '90), but finally won it in 1992.

Pat Bradley

LPGA Player of the Year in 1986 and 1991, Pat Bradley has won all four majors on the LPGA tour, including the du Maurier Classic, which she has won three times. At the beginning of 1992, Pat was the all-time LPGA money leader. Reportedly, her mother rings a back-porch bell after each Pat Bradley victory.

Betsy King

During her first seven years on the LPGA Tour (1977-83), Betsy King didn't register a single win, but she caught fire in 1984. By the close of 1990, she had won twenty-three tournaments, more than any other player on the Tour. She was in front of the money winners in 1984 and 1989 and was Player of the Year in both years. She won the Nabisco Dinah Shore in 1987, the U.S. Women's Open in 1989, and the next year she captured both titles. With the closing of 1993, Betsy's career earnings had topped $3.3 million.

The world of golf recognizes both men and women champions. And rightly so. The Bible, too, honors champions—men and women of faith. Hebrews 11, often called the Hall of Faith chapter, commends Sara as well as Abraham; Moses' mother as well as his father; Rahab; and other women. God's champions are not restricted to one gender.

Read Hebrews 11 today. As you read this Hall of Faith passage, you may want to sing "Faith of Our Mothers" as well as "Faith of Our Fathers."

16 ❑ GOLFING with a FUTURE WOMEN'S AMATEUR CHAMPION

I was fifteen when I first heard about a teenager who was attracting attention in Ontario as an excellent player. Those who knew her predicted a bright future for her in golf. I was told that her name was Marlene Stewart, and it was suggested that I play a round of golf with her at her home course in nearby Fonthill, Ontario.

I have long since forgotten who arranged our game, but I have not forgotten my impressions of Marlene. She seemed to be a wholesome and unpretentious teenager. Petite, energetic, and friendly, Marlene seemed like everybody's Miss Congeniality.

I have also long since forgotten whether Marlene or I posted the winning score that day, more than forty years ago. Likely, my memory lapse indicates that she won the game. (Repressed memory syndrome?) I do recall that she played far better than I would have expected. Consistency and accuracy marked her game.

A couple years later (1953), Marlene won the Ladies' British Amateur. In 1954 and '55 she won the Canadian Women's Amateur. In 1956 she bagged both the Canadian Women's Amateur and the U.S. Women's Amateur. Later she won the Canadian Women's Amateur repeatedly (1958, '59, '63, '68, '69, '72, and '73).

Marlene had practiced long and hard to become a champion golfer, and her championships proved that her discipline had been well invested.

The apostle Paul must have enjoyed athletic competition.

He certainly drew from the world of sports in his writings. As a disciplined and dedicated Christian, he valued the discipline and hard work athletes of his day expended in the pursuit of excellence and victors' crowns. In 1 Corinthians 9:24-27 he urged all believers to give their personal best and to gain an imperishable crown.

Read 1 Corinthians 9:24-27. In your pursuit of spiritual excellence, do you find time wasters that you need to relinquish? What do you believe God wants you to accomplish this week? this month? this year? in the next five years? Successful Christian living requires a plan that works and believers who work that plan. The Bible unfolds the plan; the believer follows it to victory.

17 ❑ THE MULLIGAN: GOLF'S GRACE GIFT

I don't know where I'd be without the mulligan. Okay, I con-fess—I do know. I'd be thirty feet off the tee box or in deep rough or out of bounds or in a water hazard or behind a ball washer.

Please don't think I need a mulligan on every hole. But a mulligan sure comes in handy once or twice during every eighteen holes. One or two mulligans have a wonderful effect on a fat score.

A mulligan is a bad tee shot that doesn't count. Without penalty, a player may hit a second tee shot and forget that the first one happened. Although it isn't allowed under *The Rules of Golf,* among friends a mulligan is often the "blest tie that binds our hearts." Generally, they agree together to allow each of them one mulligan per nine holes, on any hole except a par three. A less generous rule permits a mulligan only for the first hole.

No one can say for sure how the mulligan originated. Some golf historians claim it owes its beginning to someone's willingness to show kindness to an Irishman with a wild golf game. At any rate, the mulligan is a product of sheer, undeserved kindness. It can't be earned; it can only be received. It is golf's grace gift!

Christians know and appreciate grace. We have been saved by grace, and grace supplies all we need for living joyfully and produc-tively. Under the "rules of law," none of us deserve salvation or God's care, but divine grace sprang from God's love and kindness to embrace us and to draw us into God's family forever. Because

Jesus Christ died for our sins and arose from the grave, God has extended His grace to erase our sins and to give us a fresh start and an eternal hope.

"Amazing Grace" is more than a hymn; it is an eternal truth. Read Romans 6:17-23 and Ephesians 2:1-10. Reflect on the power of God's grace in erasing all your sins. Reflect, as well, on the purpose of His grace in making your life beautiful and honoring to Him.

18 ❑ ALLOWING for the WIND

Windy conditions challenge even the best golfers. Hitting into a strong headwind toward a green that lies just beyond a lake, players who use less club than they need will most likely make a big splash—but the wrong kind of splash. Players who use too much club when approaching a green with the wind to their backs will most likely play their next shot to the green from the opposite direction. Hooks, slices, draws, and fades are subject to the will of the wind unless players allow for the wind.

Selecting the right club is crucial when battling windy conditions. For example, you may need to add one club for every ten-mph headwind. It is also crucial to know how to hit a low shot into a headwind. Tee your ball slightly lower than normal, play it back slightly in your stance, and don't try to kill it. To take advantage of a tailwind, again, don't try to kill the ball. Tee it a little higher than normal, play it slightly ahead of your left heel, and swing normally. When facing a left-to-right crosswind, a draw shot to the green is probably your safest route to the green. Using a lighter-than-usual grip farther down the club than usual, direct your backswing inside the target line and keep it fairly flat. To compensate for a right-to-left crosswind, use a fade shot. Take an open stance, swing back outside the target line, and cut across the ball.

The book of Acts reports that the church began its existence in windy conditions. As the believers were praying together in an upper room, the sound of a rushing mighty wind permeated the room. Then the Holy Spirit filled them, empowering them to speak in foreign languages—languages they had not studied. Soon, thousands of Jews who had traveled from many foreign countries to Jerusalem for religious observances were hearing about God's wonderful works in their native languages. Three thousand Jews believed on Christ in one day.

The Hebrew word for Spirit, *ruach,* means wind or breath.

The Greek counterpart, *pneuma,* also means wind or breath. Just as the Holy Spirit swept over the early church like wind, so today He is sweeping over the church, influencing her direction. Although He dwells in every Christian, He does not force His influence on any Christian. Each believer must choose to be controlled by Him (Eph. 5:18). Those who resist His influence will struggle at best to lead a peaceful and productive life. Those who yield to His influence will experience His peace and power.

Galatians 5:16-26 describes two contrasting lifestyles. A life void of the Spirit's presence and influence offends God and injures humans. A life filled with the Spirit pleases God and displays the gracious qualities of Christ. Meditate on Galatians 5:16-26 today, and in every decision and action "allow for the Wind."

Course Number 3:
Singing Hills

For you shall go out with joy,
And be led out with peace;
The mountains and the hills
Shall break forth into singing before you,
And all the trees of the field shall clap their hands.
Isaiah 55:12

1 ❑ THE HARDEST THING in GOLF

The pros make everything in golf look so easy, don't they? They take such unhurried, easy swings, and yet their drives demonstrate accuracy and long distance. Only rarely do they find themselves in the rough, but even then their next shot is clean and accurate. Even hitting out of sand traps doesn't unnerve the pros. They are able to blast out and land within short putting distance of the cup.

Such ease and accuracy makes us wonder, *Does a pro find any aspect of golf hard?* Let's let golfing great Ray Floyd answer that question. After winning the Senior Tour Championship in Myrtle Beach, South Carolina, in November of 1994, Floyd talked about "the hardest thing in golf."

At Myrtle Beach Floyd had trailed Jim Albus by six strokes at one point, but by the end of the next ten holes he had evened the score. Then, thirteen holes later he had captured the championship. Making up such a deficit and seizing the come-from-behind victory must have been hard. But did Ray Floyd say it was the hardest thing in golf? No. He volunteered: "The hardest thing in golf is playing with a big lead. I know. I've been there. He [Jim Albus] was the only one on the golf course with any pressure on him."

When the believer appears to be far ahead of anything and anyone who would try to defeat him, he is most vulnerable. That's when the pressure is on. That's when it's hardest to maintain a life of faith.

Watching Elijah successfully confront the prophets of Baal and challenge a multitude of backslidden Israelites to return to Jehovah (1 Kings 18:18-35), one would have concluded that Elijah would always experience spiritual victory. That opinion would have grown even stronger upon hearing Elijah urge God to vindicate Himself in the eyes of His backslidden people (vv. 36-37). It would have cemented upon seeing how God answered Elijah's prayer. He swooshed fire down from heaven that consumed not only Elijah's water-doused sacrifice but also the altar and the water that had filled the trench around the altar (v. 38). No one would have dreamed then that the next day Elijah would pray to die (1 Kings 19:1-4). But Elijah had found to his dismay that the hardest thing in a life of faith is to hold on to a big lead.

The Christian is most vulnerable to defeat when he seems to hold a big lead over temptation and doubting. The apostle Paul warned that the believer who thinks he stands invincible ought to "take heed lest he fall" (1 Cor. 10:12). He recognized that the biggest fall from victory may occur in a safe zone! Read Matthew 26:31-35, 57, 67-75. Trust Christ for spiritual victory today. Trust Him tomorrow. Trust Him every day.

2 ❑ No One's Perfect—Not Even in Golf

Sports competition teaches participants many valuable lessons, but none greater than the lesson that no one is perfect. In football, place kickers sometimes miss a do-or-die field goal. In Olympic ice-skating a graceful athlete may mess up a triple axel and land ungracefully on his or her derriere. In basketball a player may miss an easy layup or a slam dunk. In golf a player may hit the hole only to see his or her ball spin out. That's what happened to Fred Couples, and it represented a $120,000 loss.

Playing the Skins Game and chipping for a birdie at the seventeenth, Couples watched helplessly as his twenty-foot chip hit the hole, spun around, and came back out. If it had stayed in the hole, Couples would have collected $120,000. Disappointed, he turned away from the hole and tossed his sand wedge into a pond.

So, nobody's perfect. Anyone who can't be happy unless he plays perfect golf had better take up a different pastime. Golf will always irritate perfectionists. Even the biggest money winners will leave a ball on the lip of a cup or catch some sand or misread a green.

God is perfect, of course, but He doesn't expect us to achieve perfection this side of heaven. Anyone who believes he has attained perfection already or has perfection within his reach needs to adjust his thinking. His theology is imperfect. The apostle John explained in 1 John 1:8 that we deceive ourselves if we insist that we have no sin.

No, God doesn't expect us to be perfect as long as we live in an imperfect world, but He does expect us to strive to be the best we can be by His grace. Read Hebrews 5:5-6:3. Observe that the perfect Savior wants us to aim for perfection and to draw progressively closer to it. Occasional slipups and spinouts may slow our spiritual journey, but nothing will stop us from arriving in heaven—perfect and happier than if we had just won golf's Skins Game.

3 ❑ A HOLE in ONE, THEN SUDDEN DEATH

Have you ever scored a hole in one? Most golfers will never realize that accomplishment. Emil Kijek was seventy-nine years old when he hit his first hole in one, but he didn't get the chance to tell about it in the clubhouse. You see, Emil fell dead at the next tee.

Many passages of Scripture warn that life is brief and uncertain. No one can lock in a guaranteed number of years. Proverbs 27:1 cautions us not to boast about tomorrow, because we don't know what tomorrow may bring. The apostle James compared human life to a vapor that appears for a brief moment and then vanishes (James 4:14). Jesus told about a self-confident rich farmer who thought the future was his to enjoy, but suddenly God recalled his soul. The rich farmer's future didn't extend even to the dawn of the next day (Luke 12:20).

Because life is so uncertain, none of us should put off doing something truly significant—something far greater than hitting a hole in one—before we die. That significant accomplishment (by God's grace) may involve the introduction of a friend, relative, or business associate to Jesus Christ. It may involve leading a Bible study or helping to construct a church building in Jamaica or reaching out to the homeless with God's love in some tangible way.

It may involve breaking down walls that have divided family members. Whatever God wants us to do is significant, but we must not assume that we can do it tomorrow.

Psalm 90:10 and 12 summon us to value every day of our brief journey through life. Moses, the writer of this psalm, prayed:

> *The days of our lives are seventy years;*
> *And if by reason of strength they are eighty years,*
> *Yet their boast is only labor and sorrow;*
> *For it is soon cut off, and we fly away. . . .*
> *So teach us to number our days,*
> *That we may gain a heart of wisdom.*

Confirm in your thinking the urgency of now by reading Ecclesiastes 3:1-15.

4 ☐ ARNOLD PALMER'S RISE to FAME

W ilfred Palmer, once golf pro at LaTrobe Country Club in the hills of Pennsylvania, would often take Arnie, his three-year-old little boy, for a tractor ride up and down LaTrobe's fairways. He could not have known then that Arnie would fall in love with golf and that golf would fall in love with Arnie. But that's exactly what happened. For more than three decades Arnold Palmer has held a special place in the hearts of millions of golfers worldwide.

When Arnold was five years old, he played golf using a cut-down-to-size ladies' iron. His game grew stronger and better as he grew taller and older. Before turning twenty he won the Western Pennsylvania Amateur. By age thirty he had won the Ohio Amateur, the U.S. Amateur, Canadian Open, Panama Open, Columbia Open, Insurance City Open, Eastern Open, Houston Open, San Diego Open, Azalea Open, Rubber City Open, St. Petersburg Open, Masters, Pepsi Open, Thunderbird Invitational, Oklahoma City Open, and West Palm Beach Open.

By 1968 and not yet forty, Arnold Palmer had won four Masters, two British Opens, one U.S. Open, and many more tournaments. His rise to fame as an aggressive-style player captured a huge, devoted following, and the distinction of being the first golfer to exceed $1 million in career winnings. In 1970 he was named athlete of the decade by the Associated Press. He may very well be athlete of the century in the hearts of many.

We must not underestimate the potential that God has built into young children. Arnie Palmer was introduced to golf at age three aboard his father's tractor, but he became famous as a golf pro who boarded jets to distant places and carried off coveted championships. Recognizing the worth and potential of children, Jesus cautioned adults not to offend or reject any child. He stressed the seriousness of this word of caution by stating that it would be better to be cast into the sea with a millstone tied around one's neck than to offend a little child (Matt. 18:6).

Read Matthew 18:1-6. Consider how many children need the kind of positive direction that Christians can provide. Kids are not troublesome little rug rats, but gifted little human beings whom God treasures. Perhaps a word of kindness spoken by a Christian to a neighborhood kid will help to build a positive concept of God. A kind deed may help that child see Christ and believe on Him. Big spiritual dividends may come from even the smallest ministry to a little child. You may not be able to give a child a tractor ride around a golf course, but you may be able to minister to him in a way that will give him a lift for life!

5 ❑ ARNIE'S ARMY

A combined go-for-it style of golf and a captivating personality drew fans to Arnold Palmer as convincingly as a powerful magnet picks up nails. Even without the growing influence of televised golf in the prime of his career, Arnold would have attracted many loyal fans. But if we factor in the magic of TV coverage, we can see how the number of his fans multiplied to become an army—"Arnie's Army."

The first division of the "Army" was clearly in place for the 1960 U.S. Open at Cherry Hills Country Club, Denver, Colorado. Two months earlier, Arnie had won the Masters at Augusta by a stroke. Now he needed another dramatic effort. And with the help of his army, Arnie was prepared to battle his way to victory.

After three rounds at Cherry Hills, it seemed improbable—even impossible—that he would win. In fifteenth place with one round to go, he trailed far behind the major contenders. But Arnie's do-or-die attitude rose to the occasion. So did his army's cheers as he launched his bold offensive. He birdied six of the next seven holes and shot a 30 on the front nine, finishing with a seventy-two-hole score of 280 and the U.S. Open in his wins column.

Arnie's Army did not have to beg for volunteers. The 1960 U.S. Open triggered a rapid and steady induction of volunteers. Before long, thousands of Arnie's fans followed him from hole to hole, cheering boisterously whenever he sank a putt. Each of his birdies elicited a hearty "Charge!" from his loyal followers. Clearly, wherever Arnold Palmer played, he had the home-field advantage.

Arnold Palmer's glory years have passed, but his colorful career will remain as a cherished legacy, and his army's loyalty will receive honorable mention in sports annals for a long, long time.

Twenty centuries ago, a groundswell of support for Jesus arose from the working class. Farmers, fishermen, carpenters, cobblers, servants, and soldiers flocked to Him. And many who were hurting physically, emotionally, and spiritually surrounded Him, hoping His word or touch would chase away their afflictions and vanquish their anxieties. Jesus did not disappoint His followers. Soon His following rose to the size of an army.

Misunderstanding the purpose of Jesus' ministry, fearing He might topple Roman authority, politicians cast suspicious eyes on Jesus' "army." Their apprehensions were fanned by hypocritical religious leaders who envied Jesus' popularity. Together these groups converged on Jesus, put Him through mock trials, condemned Him, and crucified Him. But Jesus' army is bigger now than ever, because Jesus arose from the grave to become the Commander-in-Chief of all who follow Him.

Have you sung "Onward, Christian Soldiers" recently? Why not sing it silently now? As you meditate on the invincibility and overwhelming greatness of Jesus, lift your voice to heaven and shout "Charge!" As you sing, "Like a mighty army moves the Church of God," determine to take some big strides today toward some victory Jesus wants you to share. Read Hebrews 2:9-18 and 2 Timothy 2:3-4.

6 ❑ GOLF BALL COLORS

---

olf is a colorful sport. Brightly colored golf bags, striped umbrellas of dazzling colors, and a wide variety of colored golf wear adorn every course. Why, even a golfer's language may be colorful when his temper turns red-hot upon hitting a bad shot into green trees, blue water, or brown sand. Christians, of course, say "My goodness," or something like that, at such times. A couple of decades ago, golf balls of various colors were introduced to golf, giving this artistic game additional hues.

Golf balls of various colors did not receive a unanimous welcome though. Traditionalists bellowed that their fathers, grandfathers, and great grandfathers had used only white golf balls, and they vowed that to the death they would use only white golf balls. As far as they were concerned, using an orange golf ball was a breech of golf etiquette, and using a yellow ball was downright sacrilegious. Cynics muttered that if golfers wanted to use colored golf balls they should have stuck to miniature golf. After awhile, though, golf balls of several colors gained acceptance. Today, yellow, orange, lime, and pink golf balls are hit by many golfers hoping for shots that land far down the center of a green fairway.

There certainly is nothing drab about God's way of doing things. When He created Earth, He gave it the appearance of a big blue marble (or should I say "big blue golf ball"?). Then, as the master painter, He dabbed, swabbed, stroked, and splashed vivid colors everywhere. From goldfish to golden sunsets, from butterflies to bluebirds, from peacocks to pansies, His colorful artistry is exhibited.

People, too, come in a variety of colors, and every person is the product of God's creative genius. Also, regardless of a person's color, he or she is the object of God's love. "Red and yellow, black and white; they are precious in His sight," is more than a Sunday school chorus; it is a profound theological truth. John 3:16 relates God's unconditional love of the whole world as well as His unconditional promise to bestow everlasting life on all who believe. He is an equal-opportunity Creator and Redeemer.

Racial prejudice and bigotry ought to be as foreign to Christians as Mars is to Earth. In Christ all believers are one and codependent on one another for spiritual vitality. A golfer may choose only one color when he selects golf balls, but when God uses His people, He doesn't restrict His choice to one color. Read 1 Corinthians 12:4-27, and thank God for His colorful creation and for His colorful new creation, the Church.

7 ❑ COLLECTING LOGO GOLF BALLS

few years ago, I began collecting logo golf balls. A logo, as you may know, is an identifying mark or motto. It usually features an attractively designed symbol or initials and a name. Major sports teams are readily identified by their logos. So are major industries. My logo golf ball collection includes such teams as the Chicago Cubs, the Buffalo Bills, the Chicago White Sox, the Chicago Bulls, the Chicago Bears, the Colorado Rockies, the Denver Nuggets, the Seattle Supersonics, the Milwaukee Bucks, the Colorado University Buffaloes, and the Kansas University Jayhawks. It also features businesses and golf courses.

I have to confess having a sentimental attachment to some of my logo golf balls. I added the Chicago Bulls logo ball to my collection when Michael Jordan led the Bulls to their third NBA Championship. Chicago was where I hung my golf hat during those years. I treasure the Cherry Hills logo golf ball. Cherry Hills, Denver, is where Arnold Palmer won the U.S. Open in 1960, capturing victory from the jaws of defeat. Denver was my family's home for nineteen years. My Gleneagles ball displays an eagle, colored green. I picked it up in Manchester, Vermont, when I was speaking nearby at a prophecy conference. The October foliage at Gleneagles was breathtaking. The Mickey Mouse logo golf ball holds special significance, because it often challenges me to play better than "Mickey Mouse" golf. The Arrowhead Golf Club logo ball features a sketch of majestic red rock jutting up toward blue sky. My daughter Heather, son-in-law Brad, and granddaughter Jessica live near Arrowhead, southwest of Denver, so my thoughts often fly away to their home when I pick up the Arrowhead golf ball.

As diverse and many as logo golf balls may be, their diversity and number can't compare to the diversity and number of believers scattered around the world. Yet, for all our differences, each of us is distinct and cherished by our heavenly Father. He has collected us into His family, and He knows each of us by name and has specific thoughts about each of us. Our logo may be Jim, or Jesse, or Tamara, or Tom, or Hernandez, or Hans, or Brenda, or Bob, or some other name, but what is most important is this: He calls each of us His child.

It is comforting to realize that the Lord knows each of us by name and directs His thoughts toward us. Ponder deeply the phenomenon that you belong to the Lord and are the object of His constant interest. Read Psalm 40:17; Isaiah 45:1-3; Jeremiah 29:11; and John 10:3. God has stamped His logo on your life. Carry it humbly and display it clearly.

8 ❑ GOLF BALL for SALE: $750

As a member of the Golf Collectors Society, I receive many interesting catalogs listing a vast assortment of golf items. Some catalogs offer a wide assortment of collectibles, including old golf clubs and old golf balls. It is not unusual to find clubs priced at several hundred dollars each and golf balls priced at thirty dollars each. Occasionally, the price is set even higher for a particularly rare club or ball.

I find that thumbing through golf collectibles is an entertaining way to spend an evening. Like most collectors born before World War II, I can remember clubs and balls similar to some described in the catalogs. I can't help thinking, "If only I had kept my Silver King golf balls or my caddie badges!" However, I think it would take at least a hundred years of hanging on to an old golf ball before it would command a price like the one I saw in a recent catalog. It was $750.

The $750 golf ball is an eclipse-type, patterned composition, gutty in near-mint condition. I suppose somebody will purchase it, thinking it is a bargain at $750. And it may be a bargain, but one that I can't afford.

Isn't it fascinating how we discard some old things, feeling that they are worthless, while we attach increasing value to other old things? And as we ourselves grow older, we tend to rearrange the values we attach to our possessions and relationships. We may no longer value an old floor lamp, but we value an old friend more than ever. That old photo of a movie star probably seems worthless, but the photo of Mom and Dad is priceless now that they are gone.

Here are some "items" I prize highly, and the more time passes, the more their value increases:

- The memory of Scottish parents, who never lost their brogue or their sacrificial love for their children.
- My wife. Since our marriage in 1958, she has accompanied me through a lifetime of ministry in two countries and five states. (And she has never objected to my playing golf!)
- Our children and granddaughter. They mean more to me than I can describe.
- The salvation God gave me when I trusted in His Son January 18, 1952.
- Christian friends, many of whom still call me "Pastor."
- A Bible presented to me in 1960 by the church that ordained me. Many of its pages are torn and some are partially missing, but I cherish it deeply.
- The privilege of living and worshiping in a free country.
- The privilege of fellowshiping with Christ and of serving Him.

Read Ecclesiastes 12 and Matthew 6:19-21. Take personal inventory of the things you value most highly. Are the price tags accurate? If you need to switch some tags, do it now. Opt for the things that outlast time and embrace eternity.

9 ❑ TOURNAMENT for the BLIND

B lind holes are always exciting to play, but they often wreak havoc on a scorecard. No matter how you slice it, trying to hit a hidden green is hardly a welcome task. Can you fathom, then, how difficult golf must be for the sightless? To a sightless golfer, every green is hidden and every shot is made in darkness. Nevertheless, some sightless golfers love to play golf and do so remarkably well.

When I was a young teen, a tournament for the blind was held at my home course, and I volunteered to caddie for one of the players. Ed was tall and thin and appeared to be in his forties. He possessed a quick sense of humor and a competitive spirit. He didn't win the tournament, but he showed me that he had a champion's heart. I have yet to learn of a champion with more determination and courage than Ed exhibited.

I lined Ed up for every shot, selected each club for him, and offered whatever advice I thought might be helpful. On each green, again I lined him up, told him how far he was from the hole, and advised him whether the green was fast or slow. Then I manned the flag, rattling it around in the hole so he could putt to the sound.

When he hit a good tee shot, Ed shouted with delight. When he sank a putt, he hopped with glee. But, when he muffed a shot or putted poorly, he muttered and shook his head despairingly. In those respects, he was a typical golfer indulging his fantasies and frustrations on a Saturday afternoon. Only his sightlessness categorized him as atypical.

We Christians were spiritually blind until we trusted in Jesus, the Light of the World. But the moment we believed, our faith activated a light switch. God turned on the lights in our minds. He enlightened us and flooded our minds with the knowledge of Himself (2 Cor. 4:6). As we familiarize ourselves with God and His Word, we gain light daily for steering a safe and successful course (Ps. 119:105; Eph. 1:17-19). However, if we refuse to depend on God to guide us, we have no better chance of succeeding in life than a sightless golfer has of scoring well without a guide. As the prophet Jeremiah wrote, "O LORD, I know the way of man is not in himself; / It is not in man who walks to direct his own steps" (Jer. 10:23).

The Light of the World blazes a trail for each of His followers. That trail is straight and narrow, long and uncrowded (Matt. 7:13-14). It cuts through the darkness of secular thought and leads away from selfish interests. Only those who depend on the Lord for guidance understand by experience that the narrow way is best. They truly walk in the light. Read Proverbs 3:5-6 and Ephesians 5:1-8.

10 ❑ TURF and TEES TELL TALES

Those tee marks across the face and sole of your driver and the divots you produce tell tales—tales that can help your game. They just can't wait to whisper that your swing is either right on the money, a dollar short, or nearly bankrupt.

If you haven't cleaned your driver since you last hit the links, pull it out of your golf bag now.

Got it? Good. Now, examine its face and sole for tee marks—those streaks that stand out as battle scars received in combat. If you are holding a right-handed driver and the streaks run like this, /////, pointing away from the hosel and toward the toe, you were swinging inside out and probably hooking to some degree. If the streaks run in the opposite direction, \\\\\, you were swinging outside in (cutting across the ball) and slices probably plagued you. If you are a left-handed golfer, just reverse these interpretations. If the tee marks run straight, you were probably happy with your drives.

Examining the divot hole you leave can also help you analyze your swing. A divot hole that points to the right may indicate a tendency to hook. One that points left may indicate a tendency to slice. If a divot leaves a deep hole behind where the ball lay, your backswing is likely too steep and your downswing too hard.

Life, like a game of golf, can't be replayed. After hitting a poor shot, we may wish that we could call it back and try again. But we can't retrieve our shots. Neither can we retrieve our past deeds and words. But we can learn from the past by examining what we did wrong and by trusting God to help us do right today and tomorrow. King David examined his past—his adulterous affair with Bathsheba—and admitted the wrong. Then, he acknowledged his sin, confessed it, and humbly received God's forgiveness (Ps. 32:5-6). Then he looked to the future confidently and joyfully, believing that God would guide his walk (vv. 7-8).

Believers cannot erase the past, but we can learn from it. As we confront our past sins and recognize the behavior patterns that led to those sins, we can depend on God for wisdom and strength to change our ways. Read Psalm 32. Notice that in the course of this psalm David's emotions catapulted from guilt and gloom to gladness. If he hadn't faced his past record honestly and contritely, would he have embraced the future confidently and joyfully? Are there some "tee marks and divots" you need to examine?

11 ❑ GOLF PARTNERS

They may not look like a matched set. They may not play like a matched set. But they are a matched set. They are golf partners, and their fates and fortunes are inextricably bound together for four hours. Together, in those four hours, they try to outwit, outplay, and perhaps even psych out their opponents. If they win, they congratulate each other. If they lose, they console each other, and each claims personal responsibility for the loss.

Golf partners ride together or walk together. They strategize together. They celebrate each other's fabulous shots and commiserate over their flubbed shots. When one of them has a bad hole, it seems the other comes through with flying colors to save the hole.

During four hours of golf, partners blend their skills, battle the course, and bond their souls. When the final putt sinks and the scores are tallied, they remember the best shots and excuse the worst. Then, after a hot dog and can of pop, they go their separate ways; and each is better prepared for challenges that he must face alone.

The Bible mentions partnerships: Moses and Aaron, David and Jonathan, Elijah and Elisha, Peter and John, Paul and Silas, Priscilla and Aquila. A good partnership between believers works wonders for both. As iron sharpens iron, so a friend sharpens his partner (Prov. 27:17). As Solomon wisely observed, two are better than one, because if one falls, the other can help him get back on his feet (Eccl. 4:10). Also, two can defend against a foe better than one (v. 12). Good reasons, don't you agree, to cultivate a strong partnership with a fellow Christian.

Read what Paul wrote about his partnership with Timothy in Philippians 2:19-21. Paul was under house arrest at Rome when he applauded Timothy's partnership with him in the ministry. If you and a friend have forged a strong Christian partnership, give thanks. If you don't have such a partnership, take the first step to forming one. Invite a friend over to your place. Perhaps, a partnership can begin to bond while the coffee brews.

12 ❑ Bobby Jones and Calamity Jane

To own a replica of the Calamity Jane putter is to own an important piece of American golf history.

Although the Calamity Jane had been on the market for a couple of decades, it did not become famous until Bobby Jones first used it in 1920. Then, six years later, he replaced it with another putter, Calamity Jane II, which he used masterfully in ten major championships.

Paying tribute to Bobby Jones and his Calamity Jane, the U.S. Post Office set up a temporary postal station at the 1976 U.S. Open in Atlanta. Appropriately, the station was named the Calamity Jane, Georgia station.

Today, visitors to the USGA Museum may see Calamity Jane II, donated by Bobby Jones. Calamity Jane I abides at the Augusta National Golf Club.

There is nothing fancy about Calamity Jane. Probably this simple blade putter would never have achieved fame except for one thing: Bobby Jones gripped it, and applying his putting genius, used it to win championships.

God doesn't rely on multitalented, highly educated, financially independent, and stunningly beautiful people to accomplish His purposes. Anyone with a humble heart and a love for Him will do. He used a scrubby desert bush to display His glory to Moses (Ex. 3:1-6). One stone and a shepherd youth's slingshot were powerful under His control (1 Sam. 17:45-50). He used a widow's nearly empty pantry to sustain Elijah (1 Kings 17:10-16). A little boy's lunch multiplied abundantly to feed five thousand, when the Master blessed it and divided it (John 6:1-13).

The believer who offers him or herself to God as an empty vessel will be filled with God's power and be used for His glory. God delights to unleash His ability through our availability. Read 1 Corinthians 1:26-2:5.

13 ❑ WHEN YOU FEEL LIKE QUITTING

Some of the best days of your life are spent hitting a little white ball around a golf course, aren't they? You savor the fellowship, the beauty of the surroundings, the exercise, the amazingly good shots, and the highly respectable scores. There are other days, though, that are absolutely the pits. The course seems to resemble an evil green monster determined to destroy you. He blows hard against your ball when it is in flight over water. Suddenly, it loses power and drops straight down into the deep, murky H_2O. Just as your ball lands in the fairway alongside a stretch of out of bounds, he convulses the fairway so that your ball bounces helplessly into the out of bounds. Sand traps somehow reach up and grab otherwise good shots, throw them into the sand, and bury them. When your putt is right on line, the green monster rolls the front lip of the cup so that your ball rims the cup and stays out.

Those bad days can plunge your confidence to a Death Valley elevation. You feel like quitting. You reason that soon you will hold a golf-equipment garage sale. Then you will look for a kinder form of recreation—perhaps bird watching. It will be easier to log real birdies, you surmise.

Familiar scenario? But you haven't quit playing golf, because at times, when you felt like a doomed loser, you foiled the green monster by hitting a terrific shot on the eighteenth hole. Success on the final hole gave you a lift and a renewed confidence. There will be another day of golf. The green monster will be your slave!

The Christian has good days and bad days. Days of victory and days of defeat. His spiritual journey takes him across the devil's turf, so he can expect to be hassled. If his faith is weak on any given day, he can stumble and even fall. He may feel like throwing in the towel, convinced that living the Christian life successfully is an impossible dream. But God doesn't abandon the Christian. He ministers to him, often by bringing a Bible promise to his thinking. The Christian's faith is revitalized, and he steals a victory from the jaws of defeat. It is enough to renew his confidence. Tomorrow will be a better day.

One day in our lives does not measure adequately the successfulness of our lifetimes. One step does not set the entire course of our journeys. Nor does one defeat constitute the history of our lives. When we feel like quitting, we receive gentle encouragement from the Holy Spirit, the one called alongside, and He renews our confidence in God. He assures us that in the end God will strip Satan of his power and his turf and that all believers will share Jesus' victory forever. Read Psalm 97 and Revelation 20:1-4 and claim the victory.

14 ❑ THE STOPS of a GOOD GOLFER

Backspin is a beautiful sight to behold. What can compare to the beauty of a well-hit ball biting into a green, just beyond the flag, and then skipping back and rolling gently toward it? Backspin is more than beautiful, though; it is a great stroke saver. Thanks to backspin, a skillful golfer can loft his ball over any bunker that lies close to a green, land it on the green, and keep it there. Without backspin, many a shot has cleared a bunker and landed on a green, only to bounce, skip, and roll off the far side of the green and into a sand trap or rough.

Contrary to what some golfers may think, backspin is not acquired by taking a divot behind the ball. It results from hitting down on the ball before touching the ground. Having been struck low, the ball takes to the air, spinning counterclockwise. When it lands, its counterclockwise rotation causes it to slam on the brakes and come to a quick stop.

When adversity seems to strike us Christians low and from behind, we may feel that God is unfair. However, He is simply applying the brakes to our lives. Without those sudden stops, we might scoot right past the place He wants us to be and end up in a mess. If God hadn't applied backspin to Jonah's life, Jonah would have found himself in a whale of a lot more trouble than he found himself in inside God's appointed whale. Jonah's stop in the whale's belly gave him uninterrupted time to rethink and renew his relationship with God. Later, the whale delivered a better and wiser

Jonah to dry land than the Jonah it had picked up in the Mediterranean Sea (Jonah 1:1-3:3).

When the apostle Paul tried to push eastward into Asia, God stopped him at Troas, then pulled him in the opposite direction. As a result of God's backspin in Paul's life, Europe received the gospel (Acts 16).

Read Romans 5:1-5, and thank God for whatever backspin He has applied to your life. He orders the stops as well as the steps of a good person.

15 ❑ Penalties Hurt

In clubhouse conversation, someone invariably laments, "Those two penalties killed me today. If it hadn't been for the out-of-bounds penalty on the eighth and the lost-ball penalty on the fifteenth, I would have had a really good score." Well, in spite of our lamentations, penalties have been in place a long time and will stay in place as long as golf continues.

Our golfing forefathers must have believed that attaching penalties to our sport would challenge our senses and force us to hone our skills. I suppose we ought to thank them for their good intentions, but "ouch," penalties hurt.

The game of life has penalties too. If we break God's moral laws, we offend Him and also hurt ourselves. His saving grace cancels the eternal penalty our sins deserve, but the natural consequences of our waywardness can incarcerate our joy, haunt our minds, and even keep us from receiving an eternal crown (1 Cor. 9:27).

King David violated God's moral law by having an affair with Bathsheba, and that sin imposed a heavy penalty on him. He could not sleep. He could not feel clean. Nor could he experience the joy of salvation. He hurt all over and especially deep in his soul. Finally, he confessed his sin contritely and sincerely, and God forgave him. But David's sin had set in motion a series of events that would rack his family and his nation for a long time.

In Proverbs 8, "wisdom" instructs us well concerning our choices and their consequences. Verses 32-35 indicate that by choosing to live wisely (heeding God's Word), we embrace blessing, life, and divine favor. However, as verse 36 "warns," by choosing to shun wisdom, we incur self-devastating consequences: we wrong our own souls. David's personal and family tragedies would stamp "Case Proven" over Proverbs 8:36.

Read Psalm 51. Every Christian has received eternal forgiveness from God, but no Christian has received a license to sin. Those who defy God's moral laws may confess their sins later, but in the meantime, they set events in motion that will trouble them the rest of their lives. Penalties are real, and they hurt. Trust God to help you play the game of life by His rules.

16 ❏ GOLF BALLS in CELLOPHANE WRAPPERS

A s a young teen working in a golf pro shop, I was impressed with the colorful appearance of the golf balls in our glass showcase. Penfolds, Titleists, Silver Kings, Spaldings, U.S. Royals, and Dunlops came colorfully wrapped in cellophane in those mid-twentieth-century years, and each one sold for less than a dollar. Today, the price might be $25, $30, or more. Even an empty box that once held a dozen cellophane-wrapped golf balls may fetch nearly $100 today.

The bright wrapping certainly enhanced any golf ball's appearance, but it added nothing to its performance. The true value of each ball was ultimately determined by what it was after the wrapping came off.

God's Word speaks against our judging a person's worth by outward appearance. When Israel demanded a king, the people selected Saul strictly on the basis of his good looks. He was handsome and tall. If they had selected their first king on the basis of how he looked to God, they would have chosen David, a man after God's own heart (1 Sam. 8:19-20; 13:13-14; 16:6-13).

James 2:1-5 rebukes those who judge others by their outward appearance and insists that God places the highest value on faith and faithfulness—spiritual qualities.

If people could gain God's approval simply by wearing the right clothes, the Pharisees would have been approved with a triple-A rating. But God's piercing gaze penetrated their religious robes and phylacteries and revealed their corrupt hearts. He accepted only those who believed in His Son, even if they were beggars in tattered garments or lepers with ugly sores. When God measures a person's worth, He puts His tape measure around the heart and not around a designer dress or a tailored suit. Read 1 Samuel 16:1-13 today.

17 ❑ LOST in the FAIRWAY

Losing a ball in a thick rough or wooded area hurts, but losing a ball in the fairway is a real killer, especially if it is a brand-new ball.

How can a ball just disappear? Do invisible alien creatures in invisible futuristic golf carts zoom onto fairways, snatch up golf balls, and carry them off to some outer-space research lab? Of course not. Sometimes a ball is lost in the fairway because a golfer's ego won't let him look for it farther back than he *knows* he hit it. Sometimes, it is lost because it came to rest in a grass-covered depression. Sometimes, a golfer walks or rides past a lost ball. Looking afar, he fails to see what lies under his nose.

The Bible teaches that human beings are lost until the Savior recovers them (Luke 19:10; 2 Cor. 4:3). We Christians understand this truth. We were lost before Jesus saved us. We understand, too, that Jesus has deputized us to share the good news of salvation with the whole world. What we may fail to understand is how so many people are lost "in the fairway," that is, in the center of our Christianized culture. Living in communities where evangelical churches flourish, where Christian television enters their homes, where Christian literature is accessible, and where Christians live nearby, why are so many people still lost? Perhaps, like golfers passing by a lost ball in a fairway, we expect to find the lost in some faraway place and neglect to see the lost nearby.

The Christian who looks nearby for the lost will find them everywhere. Missionary vision requires farsightedness, but it also requires nearsightedness. The church will have 20/20 missionary vision only when Christians search for the lost at home as well as abroad. Read Luke 15 and Acts 1:8. You may not have to extend your hand far to reach out and touch a lost person today.

18 ❑ EXCHANGING GOLF for an MBA

L ooking to boost their business-college enrollment, a university in the Midwest advertised its MBA program in *The Chicago Tribune.* The ad targeted weekend golfers and challenged their value system. They could make a significant choice, the ad offered. In eighty Saturdays, they could shave a few strokes off their game, or they could get their MBA. Course offerings included leadership, decision-making skills, communication, ethics in business, and total-quality management.

Tough choice! But then, life is filled with tough choices. We are often obliged to choose between what is good and what is best. Should we attend the church banquet or take the kids to the ball game as promised? Should we work overtime to pay off our debts early or spend that time with the family? Should we accept a job transfer to another state or stay put? The transfer would mean a bigger salary, but would we be leaving our relatives and church family?

For committed Christians, one powerful overriding factor determines their choices. It is the will of God. Christians do not live to please themselves but to please God. James 4:14 emphasizes the brevity of human life, comparing it to a puff of steam that appears for an instant and then vanishes. Verse 15 challenges us to qualify our intentions with the rider "If the Lord wills, we shall live and do this or that." The prayer, "Not as I will, but thy will be done," is basic to the Christian's decision-making process.

Read Luke 22:39-42 and Romans 14:7. The Lord will guide your decisions if you consign each matter to Him. Someone has stated correctly, "God always gives His best to those who leave the choice with Him."

Course Number 4: Pleasant Meadows

The LORD is my shepherd;
I shall not want.
He makes me to lie down in green pastures;
He leads me beside the still waters.
Psalm 23:1-2

1 ❑ PSYCHOLOGISTS and GOLF PROS TEAM UP

G olf is as much a game of the mind as it is a game of physical skill. Players can think themselves out of a three-foot putt, and they can also think themselves into a water hazard. Conversely, they can step up to a three-foot putt with confidence and sink it. They can also shoot over a water hazard without any fear of making a splash. Believing that success and failure are largely products of the mind, an increasing number of professional golfers are turning to sports psychologists for help.

According to *Chicago Tribune* writer Reid Hanley, "Sports psychologists are about as popular on professional golf tours as metal woods. Just about every golfer has a psychologist in his or her bag" (*Chicago Tribune,* 3 August 1993).

If golfers do have psychologists in their bags, they may have psychologists' books or tapes in their home libraries. The selection of books and tapes about the role of the mind in golf is expanding. Sports psychologist Richard Coop has authored *Mind over Golf.* Another sports psychologist, Bob Rotella, joined Coop in producing an audiotape, *Golfing Out of Your Mind.* Sports psychologist Chuck Hogan offers several tape and instructional programs.

As more and more professional golfers attain the level of nearly perfect skills, the player who emerges from the pack to enter the winner's circle may have already visualized the victory from a psychiatrist's couch.

Contrary to the opinion of some skeptics, Christianity is not a mindless religion. The Bible commands us to love the Lord our God with the whole mind (Matt. 22:37), to be renewed in our minds (Eph. 4:23), and to get our minds ready for action (1 Pet. 1:13). A proper mental attitude, one of confidence and trust in the Lord, can help us overcome obstacles and achieve victories. God has given us the spirit of a sound mind (2 Tim. 1:7) so we may accomplish His will.

Read 2 Timothy 1:6-10 and Philippians 4:13. You can accomplish everything today that God wants you to accomplish. Just rely on Him, and set your renewed mind to the task.

2 ❏ Scoring an Ace at Ninety-Nine

I have never scored a hole in one. I did get an eagle on a par four once, but somehow an eagle on a par three is a more highly coveted feat. Maybe, just maybe, I'll get that elusive hole in one someday. If it happens, I plan to hang a plaque in my office announcing the date of the "miracle," and identifying the course and hole where it took place. Hopefully, others will be playing with me when it happens; I would want their attesting signatures on the plaque. I don't think I would be able to handle the emotional trauma of scoring a hole in one when playing alone.

As I age, my window of opportunity for a hole in one is definitely shrinking, but I encourage myself with the fact that Otto Bucher scored a hole in one when his window of opportunity was almost closed, sealed, and covered over. Otto's ace occurred on the twelfth hole of La Manga Golf Course in Spain. He was ninety-nine at the time.

The excitement and accomplishments of Christian living do not end thirty or forty years before a believer dies. Right up to his departure for heaven, a believer can be empowered by the Holy Spirit to do something significant and exciting. Moses was eighty when he delivered the Ten Commandments. Caleb was eighty-five when he routed giants from Mount Hebron. The apostle John was ninety when he received the Revelation of Jesus Christ. God doesn't practice age discrimination. No Christian is too young or too old to be an instrument in His hands. As my former Greek professor used to say, "The servant of the Lord is immortal until his life's work is done."

Read the second chapter of Titus, and notice God's instructions for older men (verse 2), older women (verses 3-4), younger women (verses 4-5), and young men (verse 6). God is active in the lives of people of all ages, and He wants people of all ages to be active for Him. Also, read 1 John 2:12-14 today as you endeavor to honor God, build on the past, capture the present, and anticipate the future. The best is yet to be!

3 ❑ OLD TOM MORRIS

Tom Morris Sr. (1821-1908), known as the Grand Old Man of Golf, was born in St. Andrews, Scotland. At age eighteen he became an apprentice to Allan Robertson, ball maker and Scotland's leading golfer. He worked at Prestwick from 1851 to 1865, then returned to his native St. Andrews, where he became greenskeeper and professional at the Royal & Ancient Golf Course of St. Andrews until 1904.

Morris and Robertson combined their golf skills in team competition that resulted in their winning many matches. Later, Tom Morris Sr. and his son Tom Jr. became partners. It turned out to be a winning combination.

In addition to his being the first four-time winner of the British Open (1861, '62, '64, '67), Old Tom designed golf courses in Scotland and Ireland. He was the first designer to lay out courses in two nines.

Golfers today benefit from the dedication and effort that Old Tom Morris gave to our sport. It is also true that believers today benefit from the dedication and effort men of old gave to God's service. Moses, David, Solomon, Isaiah, Jeremiah, Ezekiel, Daniel, and other Old Testament writers, Matthew, Mark, Luke, John, James, Peter, Jude, and Paul wrote the Bible, God's holy Word, as the Holy Spirit guided them (2 Tim. 3:16; 2 Pet. 1:20-21). Our methods of communicating God's message may become more sophisticated, but the message still rests on the firm foundation provided by the Holy Spirit through godly men of old.

Read 2 Peter 2:10-21. As you meditate on this passage of Scripture, appreciate the writer's conviction that God's truth would survive him and would endure forever. Men and women of God are mortal; God's Word is eternal. Thank God for your Christian heritage, especially for the Bible. Share the message of His love today.

4 ❑ ANTIQUE GOLF AIDS

It may be fun to study the past, but who would want to return to it? We are certainly better off now with all our advanced technology than our grandparents or great-grandparents were with only crude prototypes. Can you picture what it must have been like in the 1920s to have to crank start a car in mid-January in a cold region?

Golf, too, has changed for the better over the years, but there were some great golfers in the past who played incredibly well using rather primitive equipment. Here are just a few of the aids that were available in the early 1900s:

- Sand containers and water buckets at tee boxes. A golfer would wet some sand and use it for a tee.
- The "parachute" practice ball. Because its parachute deployed in flight, this ball was suitable for use in a small area.
- The golf ball rescuer. This brass gadget clipped onto a clubhead so a player could retrieve his ball from water. The manufacturer advertised that the golf ball rescuer would prevent loss of ball, loss of time, loss of place, and loss of temper.
- The putter pencil, designed to fit into the end of a putter grip, would always be handy for keeping scores.
- The rubber shaft tip to be cemented over the end of a club. It was advertised as giving the player a feeling of confidence and a lower score.

The church, too, has come a long way since the turn of the century. Few places of worship today house straight-back wooden pews in stark surroundings. Instead, worshipers sit in comfort in beautiful sanctuaries and hear well-orchestrated music and sermons amplified by state-of-the-art sound systems and delivered amid subtle lights. Probably, no Christian would welcome a return to turn-of-the-century surroundings, but who wouldn't welcome some old-fashioned praying, some old-fashioned neighborliness, and some old-fashioned heart-searching?

Jesus warned that He was prepared to reject the church at Laodicea because the congregation had become complacent, self-confident, and conceited. Read Revelation 3:14-21. Pray for the church of the 1990s. In spite of modern sophistication, the church has not outgrown its need for old-fashioned dependence on God and love for Him. Genuine devotion and worship never become outdated.

5 ❏ Excuses, Excuses, Excuses

Scene One:	**The first Tee, any golf course**
Players:	Golfers Joe, Jim, Anthony, and Bob

Joe (taking a slow practice swing):

I can hardly swing this club. My back has been killing me for the last week or so.

Jim: My back's been hurting, too, but my left elbow is hurting even more. Doc says it's bursitis.

Anthony: I know I shouldn't be here today. I should be home soaking my left foot. I have the world's biggest blister under my big toe. I won't be able to pivot when I swing a club. No way!

Bob: Have any of you guys ever had a hangnail? I have one on my left thumb. How am I going to grip a club?

Scene Two:	**First Tee, an Illinois golf course**
Players:	Sebby, recovering from a stroke, has lost the use of his right arm; Walter, born with cerebral palsy; John, confined to a wheelchair; Bill, has battled neuromuscular atrophy for more than 30 years. All four players are members of IPLGA, the Illinois Physically Limited Golfers Association.

Sebby, Walter,
John, Bill: No complaints. Let's tee it up and play golf.

Excuses pale in view of the physical limitations the members of IPLGA face. If only there were some way to reduce the number of excuses voiced on a golf course! Perhaps *The Rules of Golf* ought to impose a two-stroke penalty for an excuse uttered during play and a one-stroke penalty for one uttered in the parking area or clubhouse.

Jesus compared God's inviting people to partake of salvation to a man's inviting many people to a banquet. Although many were invited to the banquet, they declined the offer and voiced various excuses (Luke 14:15-20). After receiving excuse upon excuse from his invited guests, the host instructed his servant to travel along roads, streets, and lanes and invite the poor and the physically disabled to the banquet (v. 21). However, even the servant's faithful performance of this assignment did not result in a full banquet room (v. 22). So the host dispatched his servant again, this time to compel others to come to the banquet (v. 23). He was determined that he would have a full house but that none of the excusers would partake of the bounty of his table (v. 24).

Read Luke 14:12-24. Like the servant in Jesus' story, the believer is on an urgent mission of inviting and constraining people to sit with God at the gospel table. As you deliver the invitation today, many may decline it, offering feeble excuses, but you may find one or two or more who will accept. And that will bring immeasurable joy to you—and to God.

6 ❑ HONESTY, the BEST POLICY

In golf, as well as in all of life, honesty is the best policy. It may hurt to report every shot and every attempted shot, but it hurts more not to. For one thing, a cheater has to live with himself, and that makes for rather poor company. And another thing—those who know he cheats will be extremely reluctant to schedule another game with him.

Beginning golfers may not know that they are supposed to count muffed shots or add two-stroke penalties when they hit out of bounds, but seasoned golfers are without excuse if they fail to count their scores correctly.

A friend and I played with a cheater a few times. Each occasion was unpleasant. Here's how he played the eleventh hole of our favorite course one day. Knowing that it was a 325-yard dogleg to the right, around an out-of-bounds thicket, and into a blind green, he tried to power his drive over the thicket. He failed, and went out of bounds. His second drive mimicked his earlier drive. Again, he landed out of bounds. His third drive hooked left and disappeared into a deep out-of-bounds gully. His fourth drive put him on the fairway, within an easy approach to the green. From there, he took two shots to get onto the green, where he two-putted. When we asked for his score, he replied nonchalantly, "Five."

Lying and cheating were woven into the fabric of pagan culture in the first century. However, Christians were expected to be distinctly different from their pagan neighbors. Instead of lying and cheating, they were supposed to "have regard for good things in the sight of all men" (Rom. 12:17). As followers of Jesus, the Truth (John 14:6), Christians were supposed to discard lying and "speak truth with his neighbor" (Eph. 4:25). Today, too, Christians should live by a high standard of honesty in a social order that often bends the truth for personal gain.

Honesty is always the best policy. The Christian who sticks with it may not post a low golf score, but he will certainly lower the risk of being considered a poor representative of Jesus Christ. Read Colossians 3:5-11 today.

7 ❑ GOLF and BUSINESS

W ho can deny that a golf course is often an ideal place to make business contacts and to forge business deals? Many marketing and sales reps know that treating a client to a round of golf may lead to a signature on the bottom line of a business agreement. One research study revealed that 90 percent of 401 executives stated that playing golf helps establish closer business relationships. Eighty percent credited playing golf as a good way to make business contacts.

Jesus did not relate to people only in the temple and synagogues. He touched people's lives in marketplaces, in fishing villages, in the countryside, and even at tax stations. And wherever He went, He used simple words to address profound needs. He brought the message of forgiveness and hope to those who could do nothing for Him.

Because Jesus met people on their own turf, He was able to gain their attention, arouse their interest in spiritual matters, and lead them to salvation. For example, Jesus met a Samaritan woman at a well outside her village in Samaria. She was a social outcast and a member of a race despised by the Jews. But Jesus showed by His ministry that He accepts all who turn to Him with their burdens and special needs. He spoke kindly to the Samaritan woman, promised her the water of life if she would receive it, and revealed Himself to her as the Messiah. When she believed, her joy and excitement were so all-consuming that she left her water pot at the well, rushed into her village, and invited others to meet Jesus.

Scan Mark 1 and 2 today. As you read, take a you-are-there approach to Jesus' ministry. Follow Him along Galilee's shore, enter Capernaum with Him, join Him in Peter's house there, hike alongside Him to nearby towns, stroll with Him along busy streets, and stop beside Him at Levi's tax station. As you see Jesus' love and compassion in action, you will want Him to guide you to someone with whom you can discuss spiritual business. Don't be surprised if He leads you to a golf course!

8 ❏ PAR TALK

S ometimes the English language doesn't make sense. *Bad* means *good* in a certain kind of slang vocabulary. *Cool* and *hot* may not be related to temperature. And *far out* may have absolutely no bearing on distance. *Coke* is no longer just a soft drink. *Gay* doesn't necessarily mean jovial. A *blast* may refer to something other than an explosion. And *grass* is not always a synonym for lawn.

The golf term *par* doesn't always make sense when we apply it to nongolfing situations. A teacher may write on a report card, "Johnny's work has not been up to par recently." Taken at face value, this report would mean that Johnny's work has been tremendous. After all, if a golf score is not *up to par,* it must be below par, and that's a tremendous accomplishment. A Father's Day card announcing, "When it comes to fathers, Dad, you are far above par" is meant to flatter, but the term "far above par" is hardly music to a golfer's ears. And who hasn't shrugged and sighed that a string of bad circumstances is "par for the course." Who wants that kind of par?

God's words, written in the Bible, are consistent with His character. He is truthful (Deut. 32:4); His words are truthful (John 17:17). He is wise (Jude 1:25); His words impart wisdom (Ps. 119:98). He is faithful (Deut. 7:9); His words are faithful (Ps. 119:86, 138; Titus 1:9). He is eternal (Deut. 33:27); His words will never pass away (Mark 13:31). He is the author of peace (1 Cor. 14:33); His Word is the agent of peace (Ps. 119:165). He is the Creator of Life (Gen. 1:1); His Word generates spiritual life (1 Peter

1:22-23). God says what He means, and He means what He says. Psalm 119:130 credits His words with giving light and under-standing.

Read Psalm 119:97-104. God's words can direct you in the right way. Count on His words to be par for your course today and always.

9 ❏ GREEN FEES

When you think about the high cost of green fees, it may be hard to believe that golf originated with the Scots. But I seldom hear anyone complain about having to pay handsomely for golfing privileges. A love for the game seems to take precedence over a love of money. Besides, who would deny that the benefits of playing golf are well worth the investment in green fees?

Haggling over green fees is as tasteless as stealing Girl Scout cookies. Some years ago, I joined three clergymen for a round of golf. As a rule, clergymen are extremely generous; they often spend beyond their expense allowances to help and nurture others. However, one of the clergymen in our foursome didn't quite fit the picture of generosity. Hoping for a green fee discount, he asked the pro shop attendant, "Do you give special consideration to clergy?"

"Yes," replied the attendant, "I'm very polite to them."

God offers salvation free to all who will accept it, but those who accept it must bear the responsibility of sharing the good news with others. And that's where cost enters the picture. It costs to maintain churches and parachurch ministries. Love for the Lord, however, ought to make our giving to His work a willing—even hilariously happy—habit.

God loves a cheerful giver, 2 Corinthians 9:7 informs us. When the offering plates are passed, believers ought to give generously and gratefully. God doesn't exact a green fee, but those who know the benefits of His salvation should give more than a green fee. And they should give themselves as well. Read 2 Corinthians 9:1-15 today.

10 ❑ THE TEN-SECOND RULE

Your putt is right on the money. It heads toward the center of the hole. It is a glorious putt. Except for one infinitely small problem. The ball rolls to a stop and hangs over the edge of the hole. Like a frightened, immobilized, first-time skydiver frozen in time at his or her aircraft's open door, the ball appears to be indecisive. Will it drop, or will it not drop? According to *The Rules of Golf,* a player can wait ten seconds for the answer. If the ball drops into the hole within ten seconds after coming to rest on the edge of the hole, it is determined that the player made the putt. If it drops into the hole after the ten seconds, the player must add another stroke to his or her score.

Ryder Cup player Sam Torrance was stung by the ten-second rule on the European Tour in 1990. He waited twenty-seven seconds for a ball to drop in from its precarious perch atop a hole. Finally, it took the plunge, and Torrance exulted, believing he had made a 3. The bad news soon reached him: He had waited too long. His score was 4.

God's patience is enormous, but it isn't limitless. He waited 120 years in the time of Noah for mankind to repent. When the 120 years expired, though, He destroyed unrepentant mankind with a flood. He waited four hundred years before He sent the Israelites into Canaan with the mandate to utterly destroy the Canaanites. He extends His patience today, but no one knows when He may withdraw it and judge our wicked civilization. Proverbs 27:1, and

29:1, and 2 Corinthians 6:2 underscore the risk of waiting too long to turn to God.

Read Ephesians 5:14-17 today. God's ambassadors do not know how much longer He will wait for specific individuals to believe on His Son. Perhaps in the next ten seconds you can target for prayer and evangelism one person whose soul may be hanging precariously at the edge of eternity.

11 ❑ STYMIE

olf Magazine's Encyclopedia of Golf gives an interesting perspective on the contribution of the Dutch to development of golf. The encyclopedia offers insights into the Dutch people's style of play and certain words they attached to their game. It seems the Dutch were playing a form of golf as early as the thirteenth century. Although they played on ice initially, hitting a ball at a post, they eventually introduced holes as targets. The Dutch word *put,* meaning "hole," may have given birth to our word *putt.* Also, a Dutch player would lament "Stuit mij" when he saw that an object stood in the way of his reaching the hole. Our word *stymie* may have originated with the Dutch *stuit mij.*

Any number of stymies may confront a golfer on any given day. Trees, of course, are the most common stymies. Having to hit from behind a tree has raised many a score and many a temper. Of course, stymies may confront players on greens too. Spike marks and scuff marks are considered stymies if they are in the line of play. A player may not eliminate such stymies by repairing them, although he or she may repair old hole plugs and ball marks.

Christians cannot live without encountering stymies, obstacles that lie between them and the goals God has set for them. A selfish desire to be wealthy has impeded some Christians' spiritual progress. At times a loved one or a close friend has blocked a believer's view of God. Careers have been known to stymie Christians. In golf players cannot remove stymies, but in the Christian life stymies can be removed. By faith we can put them aside and gain an unobstructed view of God's goals. Moses can serve as our mentor in this regard. Hebrews 11:24-29 reports that by faith Moses refused to be stymied by worldly prestige, sinful pleasures, vast wealth, Pharaoh's wrath, and the Red Sea. He cast everything aside that threatened his relationship with God, and he stayed focused on Him.

Read Hebrews 11:24-29 and 12:1-2. If something is standing like a stymie in the way of your view of God and His goals, remove it by faith.

12 ❑ GROUNDING a CLUB in the SAND

If blasting out of a sand trap is not the most difficult shot in golf, it surely ranks a close second. Many a shot has gone awry at "the beach." A bad shot out of the sand has been known to resemble either a drive or a dive. If a player strikes a ball cleanly and hard, it will take off like a rocket. If he takes too much sand, he will likely find that after the sandstorm dissipates, his ball will be resting near his feet, perhaps deeper in the sand than before.

Maybe sand-trap terror causes many golfers to ground their clubs when addressing their "beach" balls, although they know better. It is their way of reducing the fear factor. They are, however, violating Rule 13.4c, which prohibits the touching of the ground in a bunker (sand trap) "with a club or otherwise" *(The Rules of Golf)*. Other golfers who ground their clubs may be unaware that they are committing a no-no. Nevertheless, they stand guilty, too, of violating Rule 13.4c.

In his letter to the Romans, Paul stamped the righteous Judge's verdict, "Guilty," on the entire human race (Rom. 3:9-23). The heathen had failed to live up to the light they had received through God's creation. Civilized pagans had failed to recognize that their so-called moral standards were unacceptable to God. And the Jews, who possessed God's written law, had failed to keep it. So all have sinned (Rom. 3:23).

By grace, God saves those who trust in Christ as Savior (Rom. 6:23; Eph. 2:8-9), and in doing so, He removes the penalty of their sin (Rom. 8:1). Nevertheless, Christians are not free to ignore God's rules (principles) or to violate them. Christians are free to obey God willingly and gladly. Read Romans 6 today. Think about God's grace for righteous living next time you feel like grounding your club in a bunker.

13 ❑ THE FIVE-MINUTE RULE

ow long do *The Rules of Golf* allow a player to search for a lost ball? Five minutes. Rule 27 declares that a ball is "lost" if it "is not found or identified as his by the player within five minutes after the player's side or his or their caddies have begun to search for it."

If only every player would follow Rule 27, courses would be far less congested!

The soul of a human being is infinitely more valuable than a golf ball, and its lost condition carries far more serious implications than those of a lost golf ball. Fortunately, God's search for human beings who are lost spiritually exceeds the five-minute rule. He has been seeking the lost since Adam sinned in the Garden of Eden. "Where are you?" God called out to Adam (Gen. 3:9). Furthermore, the Bible concludes with God's invitation to come to Him for salvation. Revelation 22:17 records, "And the Spirit and the bride say 'Come!' And let him who hears say, 'Come!' And let him who thirsts come. Whoever desires, let him take the water of life freely." *The Rules of Golf* allows others to assist a player in searching for a lost ball, and God allows His people to aid in the search for lost souls (2 Cor. 4:3-6; 5:19-20). And once a person is found, God restores him progressively to a perfect condition. He restores that person to the flawless, unblemished image of His Son, Jesus Christ (Rom. 8:29; 2 Cor. 3:18; 1 John 3:2).

Read Luke 15:1-10. Seeking the lost often involves building a bridge of friendship between the believer and the lost person. The bridge building is not limited to five minutes, but we should waste no time in starting the construction.

14 ❏ BOBBY JONES on PUTTING

In the autumn, 1933, issue of *Esquire* Bobby Jones shared a number of putting tips. He suggested that successful putting depends on:

- *A light grip,* with the grasp being concentrated in the three smaller fingers of the left hand. The right hand controls touch and speed, but only the first joint of the right thumb touches the club.
- *A comfortable stance.* Jones stood with his knees bent slightly. He emphasized that each player must find a stance that is most comfortable to him or her and not insist on reproducing another's stance.
- *Rhythm and smoothness.* The motion of the swing must create a feeling of ease and comfort.
- *Arms resting close to the body.* Jones stood with his feet close together and his arms close to his body. His right forearm lightly touched his pants, but his left arm was free to keep the putt on line.
- *A long, sweeping stroke.* Jones started the putter back close to the ground, along an imaginary line drawn through the ball to the hole. He used the left hand for direction and the right hand for touch and speed.

Bobby Jones was truly a master of the greens. His helpful tips are worth their weight in gold to all who want to improve their putting skills.

Becoming a more effective Christian demands spiritual skills and constant practice, but the Gospels bulge with tips for living from the master of life, Jesus Christ. As we read the Gospels, we observe how Jesus prayed, did the Father's will, taught, responded to criticism as well as to praise, and touched the lives of many. Thanks to the Gospels, we can sit at the master's feet and learn of Him.

When Mary sat at Jesus' feet two thousand years ago, Jesus applauded her desire to learn from Him (Luke 10:42). None of us will truly walk in His steps until we have first sat at His feet. Read Luke 10:38-42 and 1 Peter 2:21 today.

15 ❑ THUMBS UP for a $50,000 Putt

A news photo shows Jack Nicklaus smiling and giving the thumbs-up sign after making a birdie putt worth $50,000. The putt occurred January 28, 1995, during the Senior Skins Game in Hawaii.

Most golfers can only guess how they might react to winning $50,000 for sinking a putt. If it happened to me, not only would my thumbs be up, my arms and my feet would be up too. It might even be a while before my feet would touch ground again. Yes, winning $50,000 would definitely give me quite a lift.

Many of life's greatest joys, though, aren't linked to money. Not even $50,000 can match their value. For example, what can compare to a significant answer to prayer? How can parents measure the worth of seeing their children walk with God? Good health is a gift from God and is worth far more than $50,000. In the absence of good health, God's sustaining grace is worth more than any amount of money. Also, Jesus taught that the total value of the entire world's resources and wealth is less than the value of one soul. And nothing is more valuable than the daily presence of the Savior. The Christian understands and concurs with the sentiment expressed by the words of a gospel song:

> *I'd rather have Jesus than silver or gold,*
> *I'd rather have Jesus than riches untold. . . .*
> *I'd rather have Jesus than anything*
> *This world affords today.*

No wonder the apostle Paul counseled the Philippian Christians twice in rapid succession to rejoice in the Lord (Phil. 4:4).

The Christian's spiritual journey is not easy, but it is underwritten entirely by God's "riches in glory by Christ Jesus" (Phil. 4:19). As you contemplate how "wealthy" you are, thank your heavenly Father for what He has given to you. And, while you're at it, pray with both thumbs up.

16 ☐ BEAUTIFUL COURSES

A rtistically designed golf courses are beautiful to behold and are long-lasting tributes to their architects. Who can flip through a scenic golf calendar or view a painting of Augusta's "Amen Corner" (twelfth hole) without longing to play such courses?

Golf course architects such as Old Tom Morris (1821-1908), Willie Park Jr. (1864-1925), Alister Mackenzie (1870-1934), Donald J. Ross (1872-1948), Robert Trent Jones (1906-), Paul "Pete" Dye (1925-) and Jack Nicklaus (1940-) have graced the golfing world with their knowledge and skill.

Jesus, the master architect of all creation, is preparing the New Jerusalem for our eternal occupancy. Upon completion, its glory will exceed by far the glory of the world's greatest golf courses, and its beauty will surpass by far the beauty of their fairways and greens. And best of all, Jesus will reveal Himself to all as "the King in His beauty" (Isa. 33:17).

Read the apostle John's description of the New Jerusalem in Revelation 21:1-22:5. Anticipate the splendor of your eternal home, and offer praise to the One who is preparing it for you. He is the Carpenter of Nazareth, and whatever He does is perfect. He cannot build less than a perfect dwelling for each of His followers. Our eternal home will never need repairs. It will never experience a power outage. It will never grow old, break up, or fall down. It will always be bright, comfortable, happy, and environmentally sound.

As you read the suggested passage of Scripture, you will learn that the New Jerusalem's huge wall has twelve pearly gates and twelve foundations comprised of various jewels. If you are like most Christian golfers, you must be hoping that it also has eighteen emerald greens.

17 ❏ A DOUBLE-BLADED CHIPPING IRON

My wife and I were browsing through an antique store in Rock Island, Illinois, when I saw a double-bladed chipping iron for sale. Since it was priced unbelievably low—six dollars—I bought it. I knew from past experience that a double-bladed chipping iron can be a very present help in time of trouble.

Although the "chipper" resembles a putter in that it has a putter's length and flat sole, its triangular head gives it a distinct look and function. It is intended to be used primarily for a low chip shot from the fringe of a green, but it comes in handy at other times as well. For instance, when a ball resting close to a tree prohibits a right-handed swing, the double-bladed chipping iron allows for a left-handed shot. Granted, the ball doesn't travel far, but it saves a penalty stroke.

I was watching a golf tournament on television one Sunday afternoon and observed a player hit his ball into a grove. It came to rest about a foot to the right of a tree trunk. Because he was right-handed, there was no way he could stand between the tree and the ball and hit toward the green. Did he take a penalty and drop his ball away from the tree? No. He reached into his bag, took out a left-handed club, and hit left-handed. The shot was surprisingly good. He may not have used a chipper like mine, but he confirmed my thinking that my chipper's value was far greater than the six dollars I had paid for it.

Hebrews 4:12 describes the Bible as being sharper than a

double-edged sword. It can reach where even the sharpest sword cannot go—right to the inner person—where it probes the soul and spirit and reveals the thoughts and motives that lie there. Equipped with the Bible, Christians have a distinct advantage over non-Christians. Perhaps that advantage is most noticeable when they get into tight spots. They can consult God's Word for a way of escape.

Read Psalm 1 today. The Bible is sharper than any two-edged sword, and it enables all who obey it to stay on the cutting edge of life.

18 ☐ GOLF'S BRIGHT FUTURE

G olf has become a major sport. It is played in more than seventy countries by approximately thirty-five million people.

Conversations often center on golf; books and magazines feature golf topics; merchants thrive on golf equipment and collectibles; and courses can hardly accommodate requests for tee times. In some areas cable television offers subscribers a twenty-four-hour golf channel. Golf has definitely come of age, and its popularity will surely increase and multiply.

According to the National Golf Foundation, in 1950 the number of golfers in the United States was 3,215,160, and the number of courses in the United States was 4,931. By 1991 the numbers had escalated to 24,800,000 golfers and 14,136 courses.

Factor in the high incidence of golf instruction and golf teams in high schools and colleges, and it becomes extremely clear that golf has captured the hearts and vision of a younger generation of golfers. Golf's future is as bright as an Arizona sunrise.

Christianity has an even brighter future than does golf.

Thousands of youth are making serious commitments to Christ, and believers of all ages are discussing their faith openly and intelligently. Many churches are redefining their statement of mission to conform with the New Testament's definition. The church's best days since the first century may be dawning. The future looks bright.

As believers examine the New Testament's teaching on the role of Jesus Christ in the church, they exult in the triumph He guarantees. The gates of Hades will not prevail against the church. As they examine the New Testament's teaching on their role in the church, they confront their responsibility to help fulfill its mission. Faith and personal accountability are the combined fuel for an evangelistic fire. Read Matthew 16:13-19 and Philippians 2:12-16. Brighten your world today!

About the Author

Jim Dyet, Senior Curriculum Editor for Accent Publications, Bible teacher, and author, is an avid golfer and member of the U.S. Golf Collectors Society. He was born in Scotland, the country that originated golf. At age three he moved to Canada with his parents and older brother. When he was six, he began caddying at St. Catharines Golf Course in St. Catharines, Ontario.

By sixteen Jim was scoring consistently in the 70s and was regarded locally as a golfer with a promising future. However, his conversion to Christ that same year turned his life in a different direction. Believing that God had called him into the ministry, two years later Jim sold his golf clubs to help fund his way to Moody Bible Institute. He was graduated from Moody in 1957 as senior class president.

In addition to his Moody training, Jim holds a B.A. from Houghton College and the M.A., Th.D., and D.Lit. degrees from Baptist Christian University. He also has taken graduate studies at Indiana State University and the Denver Seminary. He and his wife, Gloria, reside in Colorado Springs, Colorado.

Combining his thirty-plus years as a pastor and writer with a lifetime of golf, Jim has created meditations that every Christian golfer can appreciate. *Out of the Rough* is designed to help the Christian golfer enjoy a spiritual life that's up to par—or better!